ʿĀshūrāʾ

Āyatullāh Sayyid ʿAlī
Ḥusaynī Khāminaʾī

AL-BURĀQ

Copyright

ISBN: 978-1-956276-04-6
Printed and published by al-Burāq Publications.

Translated and annotated by al-Burāq Publications. Where needed, context and transliterations were added. Some minor edits were made to the translated Arabic text.

Cover artwork by Hassan Roholamin.

www.al-Buraq.org
publications@al-Buraq.org

First Edition | September 2021
Second Edition | July 2022

Dedication

The publication of this book was made possible through the generous support of our donors.

Please recite *Sūrat al-Fātiḥah* and ask God for the Divine reward (*thawāb*) to be conferred upon the donors and also the souls of all the deceased in whose memory their loved ones have contributed graciously towards the publication of *ʿĀshūrāʾ*.

We begin by giving all praise and thanks to God ﷻ for giving us the *tawfīq* to translate this book. He has guided us and without Him, we would not have been guided to the straight path embodied by the Prophet Muḥammad ﷺ and the Ahl al-Bayt عليهم السلام.

This book is dedicated firstly to Āyatullāh Sayyid 'Alī Ḥusaynī Khāmina'ī, who made tremendous strides in advancing the cause of Islam. It is also dedicated to all the scholars, martyrs and believers who worked tirelessly to promote the pure Muḥammadan path.

We want to also give our thanks and appreciation to all believers from around the world and acknowledge the team which helped al-Burāq Publications complete this work, spending countless hours to make its publication possible. Please recite *Sūrat al-Fātiḥah* on behalf of them, their families, and their marḥūmīn.

This book is dedicated in honor of the following individuals. Please remember them in your prayers and may God ﷻ have mercy on them and their loved ones.

Abbas A. Ajrouche
AbdulAmir M. Beydoun
Ahmad K. Hamid
AkbarAli A. Jivan
Ali A. Ftouni
Ali Aoun
Ali Hussein
Ali K. Amid
Ali M. Choucair
Alya Agemy
Andrew J. Kruger
Anees Hasnie
Assaad Gharib
Atia Sultana
Band-e-khuda
Dr. Abdallah Sheet
Ehssan Fawaz
Fardous M. Al-Rawes
Farzaneh Najafzadeh
Fatima M. Beydoun
Fatmeh Saad
Ghulam Sakhi
Haidar Alaouie
Hajj Abdallah Awad
Hajji Zeinab S. Makki
Hassan G. Afsari
Hussein Al-Ghraibawi
Imane Srour
Imtithal Dourra
Itaf Farran
Izzat Aoun
Kassem Berry
Kazim U. Begum
Khadije Aoun
Khalil A. Hamid
Khanum Rabab
Latife Jomaa
Mahmoud Tiba
Majid Salemeh
Mariambai
Mir Muhammad A. Naqvi
Mohamad Midani
Mounir Yamout
Munawwar Jehan
Najah Sleiman
Nawal A. Beydoun
Randa M. Alzaghir
Razia Sultana

Hajj Abou Kassem El-Cheikh Ali
Hajj Ahmad A. Shryim
Hajj Ahmad Fouani
Hajj Ahmad Sheet
Hajj Ali Chami
Hajj Ali K. Mourad
Hajj Ali Y. Dabaja
Hajj Hassan M. Sobh
Hajj Mohamad Shebley
Hajj Mohamad Ghasham
Hajj Mohamed Macki
Hajj Moslem Srour
Hajj Sami Ftouni
Hajj Wajih Sleiman
Hajj Youssef Dabaja
Hajji Adiba Hadous
Hajji Amneh Sobh-Ftouni
Hajji Fatima F. Sleiman
Hajji Fatima Nahle
Hajji Iman Elsaghir
Hajji Miri Srour
Hajji Wanda Macki
Hajji Zahiya Jawad

Sayed Abdullah Saleh
Sayed Assam Saleh
Sayyid Mustapha Shukr
Sayyida Aziz Fatma
Sh. Mahmoud Farhat
Shahid Ibrahim Hadi
Shahid Sayyid Khaled Saleh
Shandar Fatima
Syed Abid Raza
Syed Ali Hadi N. Sirsivi
Syed Mehdi H. Rizvi
Syed Mohammad Jaffry
Syed Mohammed Naqvi
Syed Munawwar Naqvi
Syed Mustafa Moosavi
Syed Nawab R. Kazmi
Syed Zawar H. Abidi
Syeda Aale-e-Zehra
Syeda Tauqeera Khatoon
Tahereh Najafzadeh
Turfah K. Sobh
Zaheer Hasan
Zakia Sultana

Duʿāʾ al-Ḥujjah

اللهم كن لوليك الحجة بن الحسن صلواتك
عليه وعلى آبائه في هذه الساعة وفي كل
ساعة وليا وحافظا وقائدا وناصرا ودليلا
وعينا حتى تسكنه أرضك طوعا وتمتعه فيها طويلا

O God, be, for Your representative, the Ḥujjat (proof), son of al-Ḥasan, Your blessings be upon him and his forefathers, in this hour and in every hour: a guardian, a protector, a leader, a helper, a proof, and an eye - until You make him live on the Earth, in obedience (to You), and cause him to live in it for a long time.

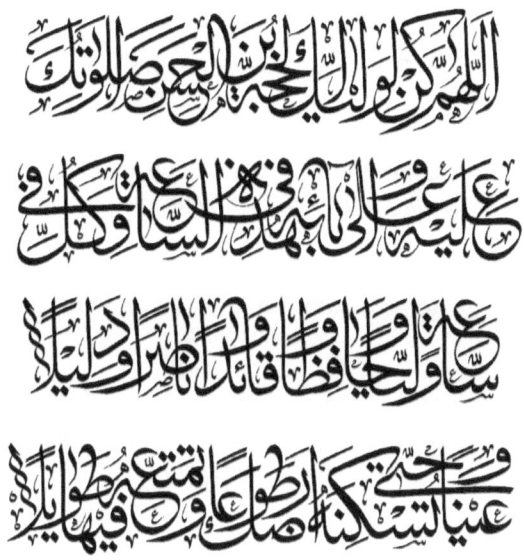

Terms of Respect

The following Arabic phrases have been used throughout this book in their respective places to show the reverence which the noble personalities deserve.

عزّ وجلّ

Used for God, meaning:
Exalted and Sublime (Perfect) is He

صلى الله عليه وآله وسلم

Used for Prophet Muḥammad, meaning:
Blessings from God be upon him and his family

عليه السلام

Used for a man (singular) of a high status, meaning:
Peace be upon him

عليها السلام

Used for a woman (singular) of a high status, meaning:
Peace be upon her

عليهما السلام

Used for men/women (dual) of a high status, meaning:
Peace be upon them both

عليهم السلام

Used for men and/or women (plural) of a high status, meaning:
Peace be upon them all

عجّل الله تعالى فرجه الشريف

Used for Imām Muḥammad al-Mahdī, meaning:
May God hasten his return

قدّس سرّه

Used for a deceased scholar, meaning:
May his resting [burial] place remain pure

Transliteration Table

The method of transliteration of Islamic terminology from the Arabic language has been carried out according to the standard transliteration table below.

ء	ʾ	ر	r	ف	f
ا	a	ز	z	ق	q
ب	b	س	s	ك	k
ت	t	ش	sh	ل	l
ث	th	ص	ṣ	م	m
ج	j	ض	ḍ	ن	n
ح	ḥ	ط	ṭ	و	w
خ	kh	ظ	ẓ	ه	h
د	d	ع	ʿ	ي	y
ذ	dh	غ	gh		
Long Vowels					
ا	ā	و	ū	ي	ī
Short Vowels					
ـَـ	a	ـُـ	u	ـِـ	i

Table of Contents

About the Author 1

Translator's Preface 7

Preface 13

The Character of Imām al-Ḥusayn عليه السلام and 'Āshūrā' 27

- Imām al-Ḥusayn عليه السلام: The Magnet of Hearts 27
- Imām al-Ḥusayn عليه السلام: An Example for Humanity 28

The Lessons of 'Āshūrā' 41

- Imām al-Ḥusayn عليه السلام's Goal: Reviving Islamic Order and Society 41
- Distinguishing Primary and Secondary Duties 61
- The Lesson of al-Arba'īn: Commemoration and the Reality of Martyrdom 67
- The Philosophy of the Uprising of 'Āshūrā'.............71
- The Eternal Sun of 'Āshūrā'.......................................72
- Sacrificing to Preserve Islam......................................82
- The Uprightness of Imām al-Ḥusayn عليه السلام and Imām Khumaynī قدس سره 83

Contemplating the Morals of 'Āshūrā' 95

- Killing the Prophet ﷺ's Son.......................................95
- The Moral of 'Āshūrā'...123
- What Caused the Incident of Karbalā' 132
- Where Do You Stand?...139

The Difficulties in Distinguishing Truth from Falsehood 172
Narrow-mindedness and the Khawārij 174
Obliviousness and Confusion Destroy Righteous Deeds 179
A Last Word in Lamenting the Master of the Martyrs, Imām al-Ḥusayn ﷺ 183

About the Author

Āyatullāh Sayyid ʿAlī Ḥusaynī Khāminaʾī is among Shīʿa Islam's leading religious authorities and is the second Supreme Leader of the Islamic Republic of Iran. Before being elected as the Leader in 1989, he was president for two terms and a member of parliament for a short period. The late Āyatullāh Sayyid Rūhullāh Mūsawī Khumaynī (the first Supreme Leader) also chose him to lead the Friday Prayer in Tehran.

His Family

On the 16th of July 1939, the future Leader of Islamic Republic was born in the holy city of Mashhad, in the province of Khorasan in Iran. Sayyid ʿAlī was the second son of Sayyid Jawād Khāminaʾī (d. 1986), a humble and well-known Islamic scholar, and Khadīja Mīrdāmādi (d. 1989) a pious and devout follower of the religion.

Education

Under the supervision of his father, Sayyid ʿAlī started his seminary education at the age of 9.

In 1957, he attended the advanced level of seminary education (*Kharij*) under Āyatullāh Sayyid Muḥammad Hādī Ḥusaynī Mīlānī. He made a short trip to Najaf with his family and participated in the seminaries of famous teachers. However, due to his father's disinclination for staying in Najaf, Sayyid ʿAlī returned to Mashhad and attended for one more year in the class of Āyatullāh Mīlānī and then moved to the seminaries of Qom to study under some of the leading scholars of the time from 1958 to 1964.

Sayyid Khāminaʾī would then return to Mashhad to help his father who suffered eyesight problems and attended again in the sessions of Āyatullāh Mīlānī until 1970.

Teaching

Since the time he was in Mashhad, he taught jurisprudence and principles of jurisprudence (including the books *Rasa'il*, *Makasib*, and *Kifaya*) and held public sessions of commentary of the Qurʾān. From 1969 onwards, he began teaching a unique course of commentary of the Qurʾān for Islamic students, which continued until 1977 before being exiled to Iranshahr. After he had become the Supreme Leader of Iran, he began teaching advanced level seminaries classes (*kharij*), and this has been continuing until today.

Teachers

Sayyid Khāminaʾī has been a student of many established scholars, some of which include:

- al-ʿAllamah Sayyid Muḥammad Ḥusayn Ṭabāṭabāʾī
- Āyatullāh Murtaḍā Ḥāʾirī Yazdī

- Āyatullāh Sayyid Ḥusayn Burūjirdī
- Āyatullāh Sayyid Jawād Khāmina'ī
- Āyatullāh Sayyid Muḥammad Hādī Ḥusaynī Mīlānī
- Āyatullāh Sayyid Muḥammad Muḥaqqiq Dāmād
- Āyatullāh Sayyid Rūhullāh Mūsawī Khumaynī
- Mīrza Muḥammad Mudarris Yazdī
- Sayyid Jalīl Ḥusayni Sīstānī

Literature

Sayyid Khāmina'ī is well versed with poetry and literature and has always been interested in reading novels, in addition to the history and culture of different nations. He remains in contact with many poets, writers and intellectuals, sharing much interest with them in an array of different literature works.

Sayyid Khāmina'ī himself has composed some poems, and he has used the pen name "Amīn" ["trustworthy"] in recent years.

Political Activities

It was in Qum, in 1962, that Sayyid Khāmina'ī joined the ranks of the revolutionary followers of Imām Khumaynī ☬ who opposed the pro-Western, anti-Islamic policies of the Shah. Despite persecution, torture, imprisonment and exile, Sayyid Khāmina'ī remained dedicated and fearless; he followed this path for the next 16 years, which ultimately led to the downfall of the Shah's brutal regime.

From May 1963 onwards, Sayyid Khāmina'ī was known for his Islamic activism and lessons on the commentary of the Noble Qur'ān, the Prophetic Traditions and Islamic ideology in Mashhad and Tehran. Watched closely by Shah's intelligence agency, the SAVAK, he was forced to go underground in 1967.

Being Appointed the Supreme Leader

After the demise of Imām Khumaynī ☬ on June 4, 1989, the Assembly of Experts for Leadership held a session in the afternoon of the same day in which some members of the Assembly mentioned Imām Khumaynī ☬'s opinion about the competence of Sayyid Khāmina'ī for the leadership of the country. Then, there was an election, and the unanimous vote of the members of the Assembly chose Sayyid Khāmina'ī as the new Supreme Leader of the Islamic Republic of Iran.

His Religious Authority

In 1994, the Assembly of Teachers of the seminary of Qom and the Community of Combatant Clerics of Tehran announced that they see Sayyid Khāmina'ī as a competent jurist for being followed by the masses. However, in a speech, Sayyid Khāmina'ī emphasized that there is no need for the masses to follow him jurisprudentially in Iran since there were many qualified jurists already fulfilling this duty. Today, millions around the world follow his jurisprudential opinions.

Translator's Preface

بسم الله الرحمن الرحيم

In the Name of God, the Beneficent, the Merciful

From the start of the Prophetic mission, Islamic history has witnessed many struggles, the first of which were the battles of the Prophet ﷺ against the polytheists and the Jews who insisted on refusing the religion and message of God ﷻ. After that came the battles of Imām ʿAlī عليه السلام against the fabrications led by Muʿāwīya's camp in Shām. These fabrications made Islamic rulings contradict their original purpose and interpreted ḥadīths and Islamic narrations in a way that served the Umayyads' interests. This was clear in the Battle of Ṣiffīn when ʿAmmār b. Yāsir (may God ﷻ have mercy on him) was killed and the Muslims remembered the Prophet's ﷺ saying, "You will be killed by the unjust group (*sataqtuluka al-fi'atu al-bāghiya*)." The people of Shām came up with a bizarre interpretation of this ḥadīth that enjoys Islamic consensus, saying, "He was killed by the man who made him fight," meaning Imām ʿAlī عليه السلام. Another example is Imām al-Ḥusayn عليه السلام who was struggling against the degradation and humiliation of the umma. This situation was actually a consequence of the reign that preceded Imām al-Ḥusayn عليه السلام. Suddenly, the swords that the Prophet ﷺ and the first Muslims raised in the face of disbelief and polytheism were raised against the Ahl al-Bayt عليهم السلام, who were the Prophet's ﷺ trust in his umma. In that same way, the pulpits that were supposed to be schools of guidance turned into platforms for worldly preachers (*wuʿāẓ al-salāṭīn*) in order to distort the basic principles and Islamic teachings that the Prophet ﷺ brought. This happened after worldly desires and defeatism took hold of the umma.

There were various opinions about the movement of Imām al-Ḥusayn ﵇. There were those who opposed him and denounced him, horrified by the blood that will be spilled, the lives that will be lost, and the division that will strike the umma. Others preferred neutrality and alleged that the matter was a conflict between two camps competing for authority and an extension of a heated historical struggle between the Hashemites and the Umayyads. A third group stood by Imām al-Ḥusayn ﵇ wholeheartedly as they believed in his legitimacy and in the necessity of obeying him. This difference of opinion is a result of the severe degradation of the umma at the time, for Imām al-Ḥusayn ﵇ was not an unknown figure or one whose behaviors and morals could cause controversy in the umma. The umma had not been without the Prophet ﷺ for a long time; surely it still remembered his love for and his attachment to his grandson Imām al-Ḥusayn ﵇. It is unthinkable that Abū ʿAbdillāh ﵇ would do anything that violates the principles of his grandfather ﷺ or demolishes what his grandfather ﷺ strove to build. It is equally unthinkable that Yazīd would champion the truth and care about Islam and its principles, especially since he is the descendant of those who did not become Muslims except when 'Alī's sword ﷺ struck them again and again, not to mention that Yazīd wholly contradicted the spirit of Islam.

If we observe the progression of Islam, we realize that the edifice built by the Prophet ﷺ has went through many periods that created a great chasm within it. This chasm almost effaced the edifice's foundation, uprooted its truths, and made it an empty shell. Imām al-Ḥusayn ؑ had to repair this chasm and return things to the way they were before. Prophet Muḥammad ﷺ was the one who established Islam and Imām al-Ḥusayn ؑ was the one who rejuvenated and breathed new life into it.

Many books and writings have studied and discussed Imām al-Ḥusayn ؑ and his uprising at length, and there have been many views and theories about this uprising. Nevertheless, it remained, in its greatness, a secret that cannot be fully uncovered.

This book is a collection of speeches in which the Leader of the Islamic Revolution, His Eminence Āyatullāh Sayyid 'Alī Ḥusaynī Khāmina'ī (may God ﷻ preserve him) discussed an important aspect of 'Āshūrā', i.e. the lessons that may be drawn from it. In truth, Sayyid Khāmina'ī's (may God ﷻ preserve him) aim was to reach the pith of the matter and warn people about the resurgence of the diseases that struck Muslim society after the death of the Prophet ﷺ.

Sayyid Khāminaʾī (may God ﷻ preserve him) is saying, for all to hear, that as long as there is truth and falsehood in every day and age, there will be a Ḥusayn ؑ and a Yazīd, so the umma must be prudent enough to make the right choice.

ʿĀshūrāʾ still contains much of what Imām al-Ḥusayn ؑ wanted to say to humanity and what he intended out of his great revolution. His call remains, "By God, I will not pledge allegiance to you like a person humiliated, nor will I give my consent like slaves." This call still echoes among Muslims, or rather throughout humanity as a whole, to lead it toward honor and dignity.

Mājid al-Khāqānī

13 Jumādā al-Ūlā, 1420 AH

Preface

بسم الله الرحمن الرحيم

In the Name of God, the Beneficent, the Merciful

Every day is ʿĀshūrāʾ and every land is Karbalāʾ

The Ḥusaynī uprising is not a momentary event limited by a space or period in time, nor is it a movement like other material movements that have limited effects and consequences. It is a divine lesson and a history of multiple chapters and components; its consequences and fruits have made it hard to deny in all times and places.

The tyrannical rulers that reigned and governed the people unjustly in Islamic lands have attempted to put out the light of this uprising or suppress it to limit its effects and uphold their illegitimate regimes. Ever since the aggressing West set foot in the lands of the Muslims, and especially the heartland of Shīʿism in Iran, it conducted studies and discovered the roots of ʿĀshūrāʾ, its effects on the umma, and the umma's attachment to Imām al-Ḥusayn ﵇. For this reason, the West made great efforts to distort or belittle ʿĀshūrāʾ.

Any arrogant, tyrannical, or usurping ruler does not like to hear of the name and memory of an incident that affects nations and leads to an awakening, a resistance of enemies, a religious consciousness, a love of wilāya, bravery, sacrifice, selflessness, and an abundance of guidance and light. The Imāms of guidance, reformers, and great scholars and callers to Islam who call for the happiness of mankind have made great efforts to preserve this uprising. The merits, lights, perfections, and miracles of humanity that have given value to its miserable history and made it worthy of preservation are blessings resulting from ʿĀshūrāʾ and Karbalāʾ.

In the contemporary age, Reza Khan Pahlavi had taken a vow to eradicate the mourning ceremonies (*majālis al-Taʿziya*) in honor of the Master of Martyrs ﷺ. His first step was to trick the public by organizing mourning processions (*mawākib al-ʿazāʾ*) within military barracks and ordering processions of soldiers to take to the streets to feign commitment to Islam and Ahl al-Bayt ﷺ. Once he came into power, he set out to implement his original mission, and he outlawed mourning ceremonies and violently attacked the religious seminaries (*al-ḥawzāt al-ʿilmiyya*) and the religious scholars because they were the carriers of the banner of ʿĀshūrāʾ. Students of the seminary headed away to the desert in the morning to be able to study away from the eyes of Reza Khan's henchmen, returning to their homes at night. The late Imām Khumaynī ﷺ recounted his bitter memories of Reza Khan's repressive measures in the period when the Imām ﷺ was still a student. Imām Khumaynī ﷺ spoke out to give a detailed explanation of Iran's contemporary history and the role foreign powers had in shaping this history, revealing dark truths about Reza Khan's tyranny.

The scheme of Reza Khan continued during the authoritarian reign of Mohammad Reza Pahlavi through deceit and trickery, as the latter used the influential media outlets he had at his disposal. However, through following the knowledgeable scholars, the Iranian people showed their commitment to their precious heritage of the mourning ceremonies (*majālis al-ta'ziya*) of the Master of Martyrs عليه السلام. Using the educational, emotional, and political lessons of Karbalā' and the Ḥusaynī epic, the late Imām Khumaynī قدس سره stirred the public's courage, and particularly that of the youth, and succeeded in laying the foundation of the greatest uprising in recent history. This uprising shattered the Pahlavi regime that acted like Fir'awn despite the global support it enjoyed, establishing a theocratic rule based on the blessed teachings of Islam. The Imām قدس سره was able to lead and establish the Islamic Revolution in Iran by taking guidance from the lessons and message of 'Āshūrā', thereby shaking the edifice of global arrogance.

The youth have learned the lessons of 'Āshūrā' from generation to generation through the processions and mourning ceremonies (*ma'ātim,* sing. *ma'tam*) of the Master of Martyrs عليه السلام that are led by preachers and panegyrists (*maddāḥūn,* sing. *maddāḥ*). These rituals documented the youth's love for Ahl al-Bayt عليهم السلام and made them more aware of the despotic measures of the tyrants of the age, igniting in them the spirit of sacrifice and selflessness.

The teachings of the late Imām ﷺ and the instructions of the Leader of the Islamic Revolution (Sayyid Khāmina'ī) emphasize these rituals' importance, as both Imāms call for practicing them in an acceptable manner without certain practices that could deface Islam such as self-flagellation (*taṭbīr*).

The commemoration of ʿĀshūrāʾ and the sacrifices of the chosen few heroes of Karbalāʾ is a commemoration of authentic, Muḥammadan Islam, for the uprising of Imām al-Ḥusayn ﷺ revitalized and preserved Islam; the commemoration of ʿĀshūrāʾ is bound to have the same effect.

As the widespread cultural invasion of the enemies of Islam grew fiercer, the Leader of the Islamic Revolution (may God ﷻ preserve him) took it upon himself to conduct a study entitled The Lessons of ʿĀshūrāʾ. Aside from his wise analysis of the miraculous effect of ʿĀshūrāʾ in building up the individual and society, he proposed a modern view of the Battle of ʿĀshūrāʾ that is a real-life manifestation of the slogan "Every day is ʿĀshūrāʾ and every land is Karbalāʾ." His Eminence (may God ﷻ preserve him) analyzed the factors that led to this painful calamity that struck the Muslim umma, entitling his work The Lessons of ʿĀshūrāʾ.

Today, Islamic reign is supreme in Iran and assumes the responsibility of guiding the umma, and particularly the youth, establishing the edifice of modern Islamic civilization and drawing lessons from Karbalāʾ and the righteousness of Imām al-Ḥusayn ﷷ. The lessons of ʿĀshūrāʾ, which have rarely received attention during the reigns of the tyrants, must be kept in mind. Drawing lessons from ʿĀshūrāʾ and knowing Ashūrāʾ fully and properly protects the Islamic order from similar incidents and prevents the repetition of a new Karbalāʾ.

Going back to the words of Sayyid Khāminaʾī (may God ﷻ preserve him), the guardian of the affairs of the Muslims, we can deduce the following lessons from ʿĀshūrāʾ:

1. The elites (*khawāṣṣ*) have a role in determining the destiny of Islamic society and preventing the disaster of Karbalāʾ and other similar incidents.

2. The conscious commitment to noble Islamic values has a role in perfecting and elevating society. Conversely, tampering with values and a weak commitment to them leads to the downfall of society and the occurrence of the painful incident of Karbalāʾ.

3. There are factors and reasons that led to the weakening of faith and the spread of corruption and vice in society.

4. Worldliness has a role in the deviation of the elite who used to support the truth.

5. The masses (*al-ʿawāmm*) do not have the correct understanding of the conditions of their time and place. Rather, they unconsciously follow the elites.

Sayyid Khāminaʾī (may God ﷻ preserve him) portrays the society that the Prophet ﷺ built on four foundations, which are clear knowledge that is free of ambiguity, absolute justice, absolute servitude (*ʿubūdiyya*) to God ﷻ that is free from polytheism (*shirk*), and love and true feeling. The Prophet ﷺ emphasized the necessity of the continuation of this path by appointing Imām ʿAlī b. Abī Ṭālib to the position of the Imāmate. Due to the conspiracy of al-Saqīfa, this was not implemented. By demonstrating the status of Imām al-Ḥusayn b. ʿAlī during his life and for the fifty years after his death, His Eminence (may God ﷻ preserve him) highlights the horror of the tragedy of Karbalāʾ in order to better demonstrate the necessity of reflection for correctly analyzing the reasons that led to this bitter incident.

In his new research, Sayyid Khāminaʾī (may God ﷻ preserve him) pointed to some companions (*ṣaḥāba*) and elites who stood by the truth at first but then fell prey to worldliness over time and strayed from the path of righteousness so much that they actively opposed it.

He issued some warnings related specifically to the elites. These warnings include:

1. The elites' tribulation of worldliness and panting after frills such as money, fame, desire, status, and position began when the companions who were present in the fields of jihād were given special treatment after deviation struck the caliphate. In order to avoid the destiny of the elites who slipped and to develop the ability of renouncing whims and worldly relationships and upholding the truth at the right time, it is important to know the world and how to enjoy it without becoming attached to it

2. The elites have to make the right decision and move at the right time to preserve religious values and divine order in society. Some elites had the duty of being present on the ground, but they made some incorrect calculations and chose to be absent. After they realized their error, they rejoined the right path, but their sacrifices did not have the desired effect of reforming society and keeping their memory alive. By giving examples from different movements, His Eminence (may God ﷻ preserve him) directs the elites' attention to the importance of their responsibilities.

3. The elites preserve principles, mottos, stances, mettle, and religious feeling. Any hesitation or weakness at this level would have grave consequences on Islamic society.

The elites must know that the masses imitate them for their unique qualities. The behavior, actions, words, emotions, and views of the elite influence the masses. This means that the weakness and the manipulation of values and the growing distance from principles is a result of the elites' behavior. The masses certainly place a huge responsibility on the elites' shoulders.

His Eminence (may God ﷻ preserve him) discusses the lessons of ʿĀshūrāʾ and highlights the elites and their effect in determining the destiny of society and their role in paving the way for the incident of ʿĀshūrāʾ as part of the Western cultural invasion that targets the faith of the umma and its young generation. He also mentions two important and related topics: the first is the intelligentsia (*al-mutanawwirūn*) and their history, while the second is freedom and the press that are subject to the enemies' schemes. By discussing these topics side by side, it may be concluded that the intelligentsia are still living in the days before the victory of the Islamic Revolution and wish for the return of the deviants of the past. By clinging to the freedom of the press, these people try to shake the umma's faith in Islamic principles and values and in Islamic wilāya. In such a case, the elites of the revolution have to determine friend from foe and the latter's weapons. Afterward, they should make the right move to prevent the umma's heart from growing weak, its values from growing dim, and its youth from having their faith shaken due to the spread of corruption, deviance, and reprehensible acts (*munkarāt*).

If the elites care about the world, material concerns, status, position, disputes, disagreement between factions, political ploys, and accounting for foreign opinions in their positive stances from the Islamic order, this leaves them ignorant of the enemy's ploys and manipulations. In this case, the right (*al-maʿrūf*) loses its glow and reprehensible acts (*munkarāt*) become entrenched. Sins, devilish whisperings (*wasāwis*, sing. *waswās*), doubts (*shubuhāt*) affect those of the masses whose faith is weak. In this case, the occurrence of ʿĀshūrāʾ again becomes inevitable, and the first victims would be the elites themselves.

The intelligentsia proved throughout its history and until the victory of the Islamic Revolution that it has failed to assume responsibility of the umma at the level of politics, culture, society, and country affairs in general. It has always fallen prey to foreign trickery, sacrificing the umma's vital interests by signing disgraceful treaties. What's worse is that it turned this umma's religion and culture into an arena for doubts and destructive Western ideas. Although the revolution made great progress in this regard and replaced this intelligentsia with religious intellectuals, the enemy is itching to return its henchmen and their chronic diseases to their former place through hundreds of ways and tricks.

Becoming alienated from the masses, abandoning religion, opposing divine teachings, collaborating with foreigners and bowing down to them are symptoms of that chronic disease that the Islamic Revolution has sought to cure. There is a frenzy in universities today in favor of Westernization (*tagharrub*). In society and in the press, we notice attempts of resurrecting the past at the hands of the subordinate and treacherous symbols of Westernization and nationalism. What would happen if the umma drew its history, knowledge, and interests from these people's words? What kind of doubts and uncertainties does the colluding press spread about the umma's beliefs, and especially among the youth and the students to undermine their faith in the basics of the Islamic order? The press presents the scandalously collaborating elements as intellectuals and progressives. What are the consequences of such an act?

There is a conspiracy underway aiming to eliminate the faith of the umma and particularly of the youth who are the source of enthusiasm, powerful emotions, political presence, sacrifice, jihād, purity, asceticism, sincerity, and independence. His Eminence (may God ﷻ preserve him) warns three layers of conscientious people in society. They are:

1. The elite: His Eminence (may God ﷻ preserve him) emphasizes the importance of the elite fulfilling their influential role in countering this conspiracy.

2. Youths, students, and officials: His Eminence (may God ﷻ preserve him) directs their attention to the necessity of caution to avoid becoming afflicted with the plagues of Westernization, collusion, and tardiness. There are agents working in the dark to return religious culture, which is one of the gains of the revolution, to the pre-revolution period.

3. Officials: His Eminence (may God ﷻ preserve him) warns them of publications issued by sinful people who have dark intellectual and political histories. These people advertise the West's freedom, which is a freedom based on colonialism, animalistic desires, corruption, sin, and reprehensible acts.

The vanguard of this invasion that targets the faith of the masses, and especially the youth, are the diseased colluding intelligentsia who follow the orders of global arrogance using the tools available to them. These tools include education, university campuses, the press, and the media. Such people claim to cling to freedom to achieve their goals. Society in general and officials in particular are the target audience of these wise warnings issued by the Leader of the Islamic Revolution (may God ﷻ preserve him). Everyone has an obligation to fulfill their responsibilities; any slacking would cause regret and the gloating of the enemies. If the situation escalates to the level of repeating Karbalā' in Iran, generations would curse those responsible and they will suffer painful divine punishment.

As we are aware of our responsibility, and in line with our efforts to write down and offer books on the elites, critical historical junctures, and the lessons of 'Āshūrā', we have gathered His Eminence's (may God ﷻ preserve him) sermons on these topics and divided them into three chapters, which are the The Character of Imām al-Ḥusayn ؊ and 'Āshūrā', the Lessons of 'Āshūrā', and Contemplating the Morals (*'ibar*, sing. *'ibra*) of 'Āshūrā'. We hope that this book will be the first step in attaining the insight (*baṣīra*) necessary to face these conspiracies with the aid of God ﷻ.

The Character of Imām al-Ḥusayn عليه السلام and ʿĀshūrāʾ

Imām al-Ḥusayn عليه السلام: The Magnet of Hearts[1]

Dear ones, the name of Imām al-Ḥusayn عليه السلام is marvelous. On an emotional level, the Imām عليه السلام has a kind of gravity that attracts Muslims. It is true that there are some Muslims who do not feel this gravity, but they are deprived of the knowledge of Imām al-Ḥusayn عليه السلام. There are people who are not Shīʿa, but many of them shed tears and yearn for Imām al-Ḥusayn عليه السلام. God ﷻ has endowed the name of Imām al-Ḥusayn عليه السلام with a special effect that moves the spirits of the Iranian people and all other people as soon as the Imām عليه السلام is mentioned. This is the emotional manifestation of the holy person of the Imām عليه السلام.

This was also the Imām's عليه السلام status among the insightful companions, and within the homes of the Prophet ﷺ and Imām ʿAlī عليه السلام. As we can conclude from the narrations and the reports of history, Imām al-Ḥusayn عليه السلام had a special significance; he was and still remains the symbol of love and affection.

The Imām عليه السلام was also special at the level of his knowledge. The loftiest truths and the most sophisticated matters of mysticism (*ʿirfān*) are contained in the supplication on the day of ʿArafa (*Duʿāʾ ʿArafa*). If we examine this supplication closely, we find that it is

---

[1] Sayyid Khāminaʾī, 3 Shaʿbān, 1416 AH.

like the Psalms of the Household of Muḥammad ﷺ,[2] filled with sweet hymns that radiate love and mystical feeling. If we look closely at some of the supplications of Imām al-Sajjād ؑ and compare them to this supplication, we conclude that the supplication of the son is an explanation of the supplication of the father. In other words, one is the root and the other is the branch. The supplication on the day of ʿArafa and the words of this great man on the day of ʿĀshūrāʾ and in other instances have a marvelous meaning and spirit. His words are indeed a deep sea of lofty and delicate knowledge and divine truths that are unequalled except in the words of other members of Ahl al-Bayt ؑ.

Imām al-Ḥusayn ؑ: An Example for Humanity[3]

Self-Mastery

Imitating the great personalities and the Authorities of God ﷻ (*awliyāʾ* Allah ﷻ) is what intelligent people in this world do. Every person seeks a role model, but not all commit to the right path in this search. If you ask some people in this world about the figures that appeal to them, you realize that they follow low and trivial people who have wasted their lives in worshipping their

---

[2] Translator's note: This is a reference to *al-Ṣaḥīfa al-Sajjādiyya*. See *al-Ṣaḥīfa al-Sajjādiyya al-Kāmila*, translated with an introduction and annotation by William C. Chittick.

[3] Sayyid Khāminaʾī's lecture on 24/9/1375 SH.

ego. Their only skill is deceiving foolish people and being a diversion for the naïve and inattentive. Such characters become role models for other people in this world. Others have political or historical figures as role models, but the smartest people of all choose only the Authorities of God as their role models. Of the most important characteristics of the Authorities of God is that they are at a level of bravery, strength, and empowerment (*iqtidār*) that allows them to be masters rather than slaves of their own selves.

It is said that a wise ancient philosopher said to Alexander the Great, "You are the slave of my slave." Alexander wondered at this and became angry at the philosopher, but the latter said, "Do not be angry, for you are the slave of your desire and temper. If you desired something or if you grew angry, you would become agitated and impatient. This is slavery to desire and temper. As for me, I harnessed my desire and temper until they became my slaves."

This may or may not be a true story, but it holds true for the prophets and Authorities of God who are divine guideposts for humanity. Some examples that may be given are Yūsūf, Ibrāhīm, and Mūsā. The lives of the Authorities of God contain many other examples. The smartest person of all is the one who takes those greats and those brave and empowered people as role models, gaining the means of becoming empowered and great internally and morally.

Among these greats and Authorities of God ﷻ themselves, there are exceptional people. Undoubtedly, Abā 'Abdillāh ؏ is one of the most important of these exceptional figures. It must be said that the light of Imām al-Ḥusayn b. Alī ؏ shines not only upon us lowly people of clay, but also upon all the realms of existence, the souls of the Authorities of God ﷻ and the greats, the angels drawn near to God ﷻ, and all the overlapping realms of existence, both those we know of and those we know do not. Whoever chooses to be guided by the light of Imām al-Ḥusayn ؏, this great sun, does a great and lofty thing.

Imām al-Ḥusayn ؏ is the grandson of the Prophet ﷺ and the son of 'Alī b. Abī Ṭālib and Sayyidah Fāṭimah al-Zahrā' ؏. This itself is a great merit that elevates a person, in addition to the fact that the Imām ؏ grew in that home, was raised by those hands, and lived in that moral atmosphere of spiritual bliss. However, he did not rest on his laurels. When the Prophet ﷺ passed away, Imām al-Ḥusayn ؏ was a youngster of eight or nine, and when the Commander of the Believers ؏ was martyred, he was a robust man of 37 or 38 years old. The reign of the Commander of the Believers ؏ was a time of tribulations (*ibtilā'*), striving, and hard work, and the receptive essence of Imām al-Ḥusayn ؏ was constantly learning from and being prepared by his father's great deeds. For this reason, his essence came out sturdy, bright and radiant.

Someone like us would have said, "This much effort is enough before my Lord." Such a behavior has nothing to do with Imām al-Ḥusayn ﷺ.

During the blessed life of his brother, Imām al-Ḥusayn ﷺ was led (*maʾmūm*) and his brother Imām al-Ḥasan ﷺ was the leader (*imām*), but the former continued his great movement and walked by his brother, doing his duties and obeying the Imām of his time unquestioningly. I invite you to reflect on every second of his life.

In the Face of Distortion

Afterward, Imām al-Ḥusayn ﷺ faced the martyrdom of his brother, living ten years after him. In other words, over ten years passed from the martyrdom of Imām al-Ḥasan ﷺ to the martyrdom of Imām al-Ḥusayn ﷺ. Observe what Imām al-Ḥusayn ﷺ was doing in the ten years that preceded the Battle of al-Ṭaff.

On the one hand, Imām al-Ḥusayn ﷺ worshipped God ﷻ, supplicated Him, and beseeched Him while secluding himself (*iʿtikāf*) in the Prophet's Mosque in an atmosphere of spiritual discipline. On the other hand, he strove to spread knowledge and stand up to distortion. Distortion, at the time, was the greatest moral threat to Islam. It was like a sweeping flood of corruption and foulness that stagnated in the minds of the Muslims. During that age, provinces (*wilāyāt*), territories, and Muslim people as a whole were ordered to curse the greatest figure in the history of Islam. Those who were accused of supporting the Commander of the Believers and believing in his Imāmate were pursued. People were killed on suspicion and taken on accusation. In these times, Imām al-Ḥusayn stood like a great mountain in the face of distortion.

The words he addressed to scholars, some of which history still preserves, reveal his great influence in this domain.

Commanding the Right and Forbidding the Wrong

Imām al-Ḥusayn also commanded the right and forbade the wrong in the best way. This subject was mentioned in his letter to Muʿāwīya. The letter, as I recall, has been mentioned by Sunnī historians. I don't think the Shīʿas recorded it either ; what I mean is that I have been unable to find it with a Shīʿa chain of transmission. Although the Shīʿas did mention it, they transmitted it from the Sunnīs. The Imām continued this method outlined in the letter, commanding the right and forbidding the wrong, until he left Medina during the reign of Yazīd. Leaving Medina itself is an act of commanding the right and forbidding the wrong. Imām al-Ḥusayn indeed said, "I want to command the right and forbid the wrong."

You see this person disciplining himself, while at the cultural level, he strove to fight distortion, spread divine rulings, and educate students and great personages, and at the political level he commanded the right and forbade the wrong. After that came his great jihad that is also related to his political role. This means that he was busy disciplining himself on three different levels.

My dear ones, Imām al-Ḥusayn ﷺ is a role model and an example, and we haven't even spoken about the period of Karbalāʾ yet. You must not pause for a moment; you must always move forward. The enemy is waiting for a breach to sneak through and is hoping you would pause so that it could attack. The best way to thwart the enemy's attack and ruin its preparations is to attack first. Your progress depends on attacking the enemy.

Attacking the Enemy is a Great Deed

Some imagine that attacking the enemy always means hauling a cannon and a rifle to some location or chanting political slogans. This is necessary in some cases, it is true, as a person must make his political position known. However, people should not imagine that when we're talking about the issue of culture, we mean only chanting against the enemy.

Of course, slogans have their necessary place, but we don't stop at slogans. One of the greatest deeds is when a person builds up himself and his children and all those who he is responsible for, not to mention building up the umma as a whole.

The enemy persists in trying to shake the stability of this mighty bulwark, weaken it, or make it vulnerable.

The enemy is Western arrogance (*istikbār*), with its ignorant (*jāhilī*), lowly, and authoritarian culture. Despite all its superficial empty greatness, the enemy has dominated the whole world and controlled its economic, cultural, human, and political riches for centuries, and today it is facing a serious challenge from true Islam, not the Islam of propaganda.

Some who pretend to be Muslims—and they are Muslims by name only—sit at the enemy's tables, orbit around it, and grovel to it. It's natural that the enemy does not fear such an Islam.

The real bulwark comes from true Islam, the Islam of the Qurʾān and of "God ﷻ will never provide the faithless any way [to prevail] over the faithful." If we want to be more precise, we say that true Islam is the Islam of "Indeed God ﷻ has bought from the faithful their souls and their possessions for paradise to be theirs." It is your Islam, you whose bodies are wounded by shrapnel and who know war and jihād in the way God ﷻ. Your counterparts are those who made sacrifices and the families of martyrs and those who fought at the front and came back safely despite the enemies' wishes. This is the main fortification.

Fighting the Enemy is a Duty

The enemy is not unaware of this barrier; it's always scheming to attack it and sink its claws into it. We, however, have to stand against that and respond to it. Moving and striving are necessary for disciplining the self and building it up; this is of prime importance. This is what Imām al-Ḥusayn ﷺ did himself, and he is your lord and master. Moving in the political domain through commanding the right and being present is also necessary, in addition to explaining political stances against the powers of arrogance when necessary. Cultural jihad is also important for building man up, improving the self, disciplining thought, and spreading knowledge and culture.

All this is a duty for anyone whose role model is Imām al-Ḥusayn ﷺ.

It is our people's pleasure to honor and revere al-Ḥusayn ﷺ, and many non-Muslims feel this way too.

Imām al-Ḥusayn ﷺ Against the World

Now we come to talking about Karbalāʾ. Karbalāʾ is important for another reason, and it is a lesson for anyone who wants to follow the Imām's ﷺ example.

You know, dear ones, that the Battle of Karbalā' lasted for a day or a little more during which a number of about seventy-two people were martyred. Although many people in the world were martyred and are still being martyred, you know about the greatness and splendor of the Battle of Karbalā'. It is worthy of such greatness and splendor, and it is greater and more splendid still. Its effects and blessings have spread throughout human existence. Karbalā's greatness is due to its internal truth, for it is not of great importance externally. Children have been killed all over the world, after all. In Karbalā', a six-month-old infant was killed. The enemies have committed a genocide against people in some places and killed hundreds of children. What matters is not the material dimension but the spiritual dimension.

The spirit of the matter is that Imām al-Ḥusayn ﵇ was not facing a vast army; the point isn't that he was battling a horde of enemies. It wouldn't even matter if the enemies were a hundred times more numerous. His actual battle was with a whole world of deviance and darkness; this is the important thing. At the time that the Imām ﵇ was facing that world of darkness and injustice and deviance, those opposing him had everything: money, gold, power, authors, poets, ḥadīth transmitters, and speakers. What a frightening, awful position, and yet neither heart nor limb of the Imām ﵇ shook. Weakness did not find a way to his heart, and he did not hesitate to go out to the battle field all alone.

The greatness of Karbalāʾ came out of the fact that Imām al-Ḥusayn's ﷺ rising up was for God ﷻ's sake.

Imām al-Ḥusayn's ﷺ position may be likened and compared to the position of his grandfather the Prophet Muḥammad ﷺ at the start of his prophetic mission (*biʿtha*). As the Prophet ﷺ stood up against a whole world, Imām al-Ḥusayn ﷺ stood up against a whole world in Karbalāʾ. The Prophet ﷺ had no fear; he was steadfast and kept moving forward, and Imām al-Ḥusayn ﷺ was also fearless and steadfast as he went on. The movements of the Prophet ﷺ and Imām al-Ḥusayn ﷺ are like two circles with one center and one goal. This is the meaning of the ḥadīth: "Al-Ḥusayn ﷺ is from me and I am from al-Ḥusayn ﷺ." The greatness of Imām al-Ḥusayn ﷺ stems from this point.

Imām al-Ḥusayn ﷺ said on the eve of the tenth day of Muḥarram, "Go. You are not accountable if you leave me. The night has fallen upon you, so make it your escape camel. Let each man of you grab the hand of a man from my household. It's me they're after." Imām al-Ḥusayn ﷺ was being entirely serious. Let's suppose that they complied and left while Imām al-Ḥusayn ﷺ remained alone or with no more than ten supporters. Would that have diminished his greatness? No, his greatness would have remained unchanged. Similarly, if his seventy-two companions were seventy-two thousand, that wouldn't have diminished his greatness either. All the pressures of this world did not make the

Imām hesitate. Imām al-Ḥusayn's greatness lies in his steadfastness and certainty as he faced a world that was opposing him and usurping his right. He was unwavering. The truth is such a situation would cause most people, even the best among them, to become confused. Like I mentioned many times before, ʿAbdullāh b. ʿAbbās, a great and esteemed personage, and all the notables of Quraysh disliked the conditions of their time, as did ʿAbdullāh b. al-Zubayr, ʿAbdullāh b. ʿUmar, ʿAbd al-Raḥmān b. Abī Bakr, and the sons of the great companions and some companions themselves. There were many companions in Medina who were characterized by chivalry (*murūʾa*) and honor (*ghayra*). Don't think that they didn't have chivalry and honor. These same companions stood up to Muslim b. ʿAqaba in the Battle of al-Ḥarra when the latter attacked Medina and committed massacres a year after the Battle of Karbalāʾ. Don't think they were cowards; they were brave warriors.

However, the bravery of going to battle is one thing, and the bravery of facing an entire world is another thing entirely. Imām al-Ḥusayn chose the second path, and his movement was for this path's sake. This is why I have repeatedly emphasized that the movement of our great Imām was a Ḥusaynī movement. In our present age, the stance of Imām Khumaynī had something of Imām al-Ḥusayn's movement. Some might say that Imām al-Ḥusayn was killed while thirsty in the desert of Karbalāʾ whereas Imām

The Character of Imām al-Ḥusayn ﷺ and 'Āshūrā'

Khumaynī ؒ ruled and lived in glory, and when he passed away multitudes walked behind his funeral. Nevertheless, this is not the yardstick. The essence is in facing a great injustice, a great vacuum, that has everything under its control. I mentioned before the money, power, men, speakers, and preachers that were under the control of Imām al-Ḥusayn's ﷺ enemies.

Dear ones, your situation today is similar to that time. Karbalā' extends across eternity. It is not limited to a geographical space of a few hundred meters. History is repeating itself today as a whole world of injustice and arrogance is standing in the face of the Islamic Republic.

The Lessons of ʿĀshūrāʾ

Imām al-Ḥusayn ؑ's Goal: Reviving Islamic Order and Society[4]

On the day of ʿĀshūrāʾ, I will be speaking of the revolution of Imām al-Ḥusayn ؑ. It is a wondrous thing how our life, thanks be to God ﷻ, is filled with the mention of Imām al-Ḥusayn ؑ. Much has been said about the uprising of this great man, but the more one reflects on the topic, the more avenues of contemplation and analysis open up before him. There is still much that hasn't been said about this marvelous and incomparable incident. For this reason, we must reflect on it and speak to others about it.

A Few Months and More Than a Hundred Lessons

If we follow the movements Abū ʿAbdillāh ؑ took from the day he went out of Medina and headed to Mecca until he was martyred in Karbalāʾ, we realize that a hundred lessons may be learned from this movement that lasted for only a few months—I don't want to say a thousand lessons, although that is possible too, because every gesture our great Imām ؑ made could be a lesson. Nevertheless, when I say a hundred lessons, I mean that if we studied his deeds, we could point out a hundred different subjects. Each subject would be a lesson to nations (*umma*, pl. *umam*), history, and countries in self-discipline, the government of society, and drawing

---

[4] Sayyid Khāminaʾī's Friday prayer sermon on the tenth of Muḥarram 1416 AH.

near to God ﷻ. Such is Imām al-Ḥusayn b. ʿAlī ؑ, like a shining sun among the saints (*qiddīsīn*, sing. *qiddīs*). If prophets, Imāms, martyrs, and righteous people are like moons and stars, Imām al-Ḥusayn ؑ is a rising sun among them, for the reasons I already outlined.

The Most Important Lesson: Why Did Imām al-Ḥusayn ؑ Revolt?

In addition to these hundred lessons, the primary lesson that I will seek to explain to you lies in the question: why did Imām al-Ḥusayn ؑ revolt? Why did you, O Imām al-Ḥusayn ؑ, revolt although you are a respected personage in Mecca and Medina and have your followers (*Shīʿa*) in Yemen? Why didn't you go to a place where you had nothing to do with Yazīd and Yazīd had nothing to do with you, where you could live and worship and preach?

This is the main question and lesson. I don't claim that no one pointed this out before; others have discussed this issue and spoken about it extensively. What I would like to say today is only a comprehensive conclusion and a new view of the topic.

Did Imām al-Ḥusayn ؑ Revolt for the Sake of Government?

Some people like to say that the goal of Imām Abū ʿAbdillāh's ؑ revolt was to remove the corrupt rule of

Yazīd and establish his own rule. Such a saying would be true if Imām al-Ḥusayn ﷺ revolted to establish his rule and when he couldn't, he said, "We couldn't achieve our goal. Let's go back."

A person who revolts for the sake of government will continue on this path as long as he sees a possibility of achieving his goal. If there was no reasonable possibility, this person's duty would be to go back. Those who say that the goal of Imām al-Ḥusayn ﷺ was to establish the true rule of Imām 'Alī ﷺ are wrong, as the aspects of the former's movement do not indicate this. I will explain this later.

In contrast, others have said, "What rule do you speak of? Imām al-Ḥusayn ﷺ knew that he could not establish his rule. He came to be martyred." This became a widespread belief for a long time, and some people expressed it elegantly. I have even heard some great scholars saying this. The opinion that the Imām ﷺ revolted to achieve martyrdom is not new. According to this opinion, Imām al-Ḥusayn ﷺ believed that staying alive cannot cause a change, so he decided to cause a change through martyrdom.

Did Imām al-Ḥusayn ﷺ Revolt to be Martyred?

This opinion too has no basis in Islamic legal sources, as there is nothing that supports throwing away one's life. The martyrdom we are familiar with in our sacred law, verses, and narrations is a movement toward death and an acceptance of it for an obligatory or probable goal. This is rightful martyrdom in Islam. Nevertheless, acting for the purpose of being killed is unacceptable. Although the second opinion contains something of the truth, it does not describe Imām al-Ḥusayn's ﷷ goal.

In summary, we can neither say that Imām al-Ḥusayn ﷷ revolted to establish his rule nor to attain martyrdom.

Government and Martyrdom are Consequences

I believe that those who say that the goal was government or the goal was martyrdom have mixed up cause and consequence. This wasn't the goal. Imām al-Ḥusayn ﷷ had a role whose fulfillment required a movement that led to one of two consequences: either government or martyrdom. Imām al-Ḥusayn ﷷ was prepared for both possibilities; he prepared for government and for martyrdom. Whichever of them happened would be rightful, but they were consequences and not goals in themselves.

A Novel Obligation

In that case, what was the goal? I will summarize it at first and then I'll explain further.

If we are stating the goal of Imām al-Ḥusayn ﷷ, we should say that that the great man's goal was to fulfill a great religious obligation that had never been performed before, neither by the Prophet ﷺ and nor Imām ʿAlī ؑ and Imām al-Ḥasan ؑ. It is an obligation of great importance in the system of thought, values, and practice in Islam. Why was this obligation never performed before despite its importance? Imām al-Ḥusayn ؑ had to fulfill this obligation so it could be a lesson across history the same way that the Prophet's ﷺ government and jihād were lessons for Muslims and all humanity. Imām al-Ḥusayn ؑ had to perform this obligation for it to be a lesson for all Muslims.

Waiting for the Right Time

Why was it Imām al-Ḥusayn ؑ who fulfilled this obligation? It was because the circumstances were just right in his time. Had these circumstances come together in the time of Imām ʿAlī al-Hādī ؑ instead, Imām ʿAlī al-Hādī ؑ would have become Islam's great sacrifice (*dhibḥ*). The same applies to Imām al-Ḥasan ؑ or Imām Jaʿfar al-Ṣādiq ؑ. However, the circumstances were not convenient during the time of any Imām up to the age of occultation (*ʿaṣr al-ghayba*) except Imām al-Ḥusayn ؑ.

The goal, then, was performing the obligation of either coming into government and authority so that society would go back to its state during the time of the Prophet ﷺ and Imām ʿAlī ؑ, or attaining martyrdom, and Imām al-Ḥusayn عليه السلام was prepared for both possibilities.

God ﷻ created Imām al-Ḥusayn عليه السلام with the capacity for martyrdom in this path, and the Imām عليه السلام was able to bear this weight. As for the calamities of Karbalāʾ, they constitute another layer of greatness.

The Bringer of Islamic Teachings

The Prophet ﷺ, and this applies to every prophet, brought forth a group of teachings when his prophetic mission began. Some of these teachings are for the reform of the individual and others are for building societies and managing human affairs. These teachings are called the Islamic order (*al-niẓām al-Islāmī*).

When Islam was revealed to the sacred heart of the Prophet ﷺ, he brought forth prayer, fasting, almsgiving, pilgrimage, Islamic rulings, and standards of personal relationships. After that, he brought forth jihād in the way of God ﷻ, government, the economic system, the standards of the relationship between the ruler and his subjects, and the subjects' duties to the ruler. Islam brought forth these rulings for humanity and the noble Prophet ﷺ explained them: "There is nothing that brings you closer to Paradise and distances you from Hell except that I told you to do."[5]

The Noble Prophet ﷺ not only explained the components of personal and communal felicity, but also practiced these components himself. He established Islamic government and Islamic society, and worked according to Islamic economy. During his time, jihād was practiced and alms were paid. This means the Prophet ﷺ established the Islamic order, making the Prophet ﷺ and his successor Imām 'Alī ؑ the builders and leaders of this order.

The way was clear and both individuals and society had to commit to it if they wanted to reach perfection and become as righteous as angels, putting an end to injustice, evil, corruption, division, poverty, and ignorance. This way, people could attain perfect happiness and become God ﷻ's ideal servants.

What is the Obligation?

A question arises here: if the trajectory that the Prophet ﷺ set deviated from its course, what would be our obligation (*taklīf*)? If Islamic society deviated so much that the essence of Islam was at risk, this could have two causes. In the first case, people deviate from

[5] al-Majlisī, al-'Allamah Muḥammad Bāqir, *Biḥār al-Anwār*, Vol. 2, p. 170.

the right path—and this happens often—but the Islamic rulings remain intact. In the second case, the people deviate and the rulers, scholars, and teachers of religion become corrupt. If this happens the Qurʾān becomes distorted, good deeds become bad deeds, the right (*al-maʿrūf*) becomes the wrong (*al-munkar*), and Islam turns upside down. What is the obligation in such a case?

A Clear Obligation and Inconvenient Circumstances

The Qurʾān determined the obligation and the Prophet ﷺ explained it: "O you who have faith! Should any of you desert his religion, God ﷻ will soon bring a people whom He loves and who love Him, [who will be] humble towards the faithful, stern towards the faithless, waging jihād in the way of God ﷻ, not fearing the blame of any blamer."[6] There are many other similar verses and narrations.

However, was the Prophet ﷺ able to implement this divine ruling? No, because this is only possible in an age of deviation so great that it threatens Islam. Islamic society did not undergo such a deviation in the ages of the Prophet ﷺ or Imām ʿAlī ؑ. Even in the age of Imām al-Ḥasan ؑ when Muʿāwīya was in power and when many aspects of deviation were present, the essence of Islam was not threatened yet. It's true that at a certain

[6] Sūrat al-Māʾida, Verse 54.

time deviation reached the absolute limit, but the time still wasn't right.

Returning Society to the Right Path

This Islamic ruling is not less important than Islamic government because the government means managing society. If society deviated and became corrupt and Islamic rulings were suspended and there were no rulings about effecting change and renewal—which is termed revolution in our day—what is the point of Islamic government? The ruling about returning a deviant society to the right path is no less important than Islamic government itself. It may be said that this act exceeds fighting the faithless and commanding the right and forbidding the wrong. It even exceeds great acts of worship such as the pilgrimage. Why is that? It's because this ruling guarantees reviving Islam though it might be dead or close to death.

Who should implement this ruling and undertake this obligation? It's the successor of the Prophet ﷺ during whose time such a deviation takes place as long as the circumstances are right. This latter point is necessary because God ﷻ does not make futile things obligatory. Naturally, the right circumstances don't mean the absence of danger; that's not the point. The point is that a person should know that his act will have a tangible result manifest in making his call known among the people, making them understand, and causing them to come back from wrongdoing.

Deviation and Revolution in Imām al-Ḥusayn's ﷺ Time

Islam deviated during the time of Imām al-Ḥusayn ﷺ and the circumstances were convenient, so he was obligated to revolt. The person who came into power after Mu'āwīya did not even observe Islam for appearances' sake. He indulged in wine, debauchery (*mujūn*), the ridicule of the Qur'ān, and the promotion of lewd (*ibāḥī*) poetry. Yazīd publicly opposed Islam, but being the ruler of the Muslims, he did not want to leave Islam. He did not practice Islam or care about it, which made him like a fountain of foul water that pollutes everything around it. A corrupt ruler is always like this; when he assumes authority, his acts are no longer limited to himself but they spread all around him. The corruption of ordinary people, in contrast, is limited to themselves or to their close circle of acquaintances. The higher one's rank in Islamic society, the more harmful his corruption would be. However, if the ruler himself became corrupt, his corruption would spread everywhere. Similarly, if the ruler was righteous, his righteousness would extend everywhere.

Such a corrupt person succeeded Mu'āwīya in ruling the Muslims and became the successor of the Prophet ﷺ. Is there more deviation than this? And so the circumstances became convenient, but what does that mean? Does it mean the absence of danger? No, there's always danger, and it's expected for a ruler to put his opponents in danger; it's common sense.

The Status of the Imāms عليهم السلام is the Same

When we speak of the right circumstances, we mean that the circumstances have to be convenient for the Imām عليه السلام to make his call heard in his time and across history. If Imām al-Ḥusayn عليه السلام revolted in the days of Muʿāwīya, his call wouldn't have been heard because the rule and policies of the time had made people deaf to the truth. For this reason, and although Imām al-Ḥusayn عليه السلام was an Imām for ten years during Muʿāwīya's reign, he, like Imām al-Ḥasan عليه السلام, did not revolt. The circumstances weren't right. It's not that Imām al-Ḥasan عليه السلام was not worthy of revolting; there is no difference between Imām al-Ḥusayn عليه السلام and any of the other Imāms عليهم السلام. Of course, the status of Imām al-Ḥusayn عليه السلام who waged this act of jihād is higher than the status of the Imāms عليهم السلام who could not wage it, but all the Imāms عليهم السلام are equal in the position of Imāmate. Had the same thing happened in their time, they would have revolted and acquired that status themselves.

A Dangerous Obligation

Imām al-Ḥusayn عليه السلام was facing deviation and the circumstances were convenient, so he had to undertake this obligation. When ʿAbdullāh b. Jaʿfar, Muḥammad

b. al-Ḥanafiyya, and ʿAbdullāh b. ʿAbbās, who are scholars knowledgeable about the rulings of Islam, said to Imām al-Ḥusayn ﷺ that revolting was dangerous, what they meant was that he was under no obligation to act due to the danger involved. What they did not realize was that this was not the kind of obligation that could be suspended due to danger. Such an obligation is always dangerous. How could a person revolt against a tyrannical rule without being in danger?

Imām Khumaynī ؒ fulfilled this same obligation. When he was told that he was endangering himself by standing up to the Shah, didn't he already know that? Didn't the Imām ؒ know that the SAVAK arrested its opponents, killed them, tortured them, and arrested and exiled even their friends? The circumstances of Imām al-Ḥusayn ﷺ were repeated in miniature in Imām Khumaynī's ؒ time. The difference is that in one case they led to martyrdom and in the other to the establishment of an Islamic government. Imām al-Ḥusayn ﷺ and our great Imām ؒ had a common goal. This is the fountain of Ḥusaynī knowledge that forms an important aspect of Shīʿa knowledge, and it is an important pillar of Islam.

Returning Islamic Society to the Right Path

The goal was returning Islam and Islamic society to the right path after their deviation due to the ignorance, injustice, tyranny, and treachery of some people, and the circumstances were right. Of course, historical periods aren't identical; the circumstances may be convenient during one time but not another. The circumstances were convenient in the time of Imām al-Ḥusayn ؑ and also our time. For this reason, Imām Khumaynī ؓ acted in the same way. The only difference is that revolting against false rule ended in establishing an Islamic government in our time, praise be to God ﷻ, whereas in the time of Imām al-Ḥusayn ؑ the revolt ended in martyrdom. Would revolting in the second case stop being an obligation? Would it become futile if its outcome was martyrdom? No, revolting is an obligation whether it ends in martyrdom or government. Both consequences have their own advantages, but acting is a must in both cases.

The First Obligation of its Kind

This is what Imām al-Ḥusayn ؑ did, and he was the first to do such a thing. There was no deviation in the time of the Prophet ﷺ and Imām 'Alī ؑ. If there was deviation in certain aspects, the circumstances weren't convenient. On the other hand, both deviation and proper circumstances were available during Imām al-Ḥusayn's ؑ time. This is the most important thing about his uprising.

We can summarize things as follows: the revolt of Imām al-Ḥusayn ؑ was to fulfill the great obligation of rebuilding Islam and Islamic society and stand up to the dangerous deviations that struck Islamic society. This can only be done through revolt and commanding the right and forbidding the wrong; it is a great manifestation of commanding the right and forbidding the wrong. As I already said, the result could either be establishing a government or martyrdom. Imām al-Ḥusayn was prepared for both possibilities.

Islam was Threatened During Yazīd's Reign

The proof for what I'm saying comes from the words of Imām al-Ḥusayn himself. I have chosen some sayings of Imām al-Ḥusayn that point out this fact.

When al-Walīd, the governor of Medina, summoned Imām al-Ḥusayn at night and told him that Muʿāwiya was dead and that he had to pledge allegiance to Yazīd, the Imām responded, "Morning will come upon you and us and we will see who is more entitled to the caliphate."[7] When Marwān b. al-Ḥakam saw him in the morning and told him to pledge allegiance to Yazīd and not endanger his own life, Imām al-Ḥusayn said, "Indeed we belong to God, and to Him do we indeed return, and peace be upon Islam if the umma was tried with a ruler like Yazīd."[8] The issue is not Yazīd personally, but anyone like Yazīd. Imām al-Ḥusayn

---

[7] al-Majlisī, al-ʿAllāmah Muḥammad Bāqir, *Biḥār al-Anwār*, Vol. 44, p. 325.

[8] Ibid.

wanted to say, "We have put up with everything that happened in the past, but now the essence of Islam and Islamic order are at risk." This means that deviation is a real threat. The issue is a danger that threatens the essence of Islam.

Imām al-Ḥusayn ؑ addressed two testaments to his brother Muḥammad b. al-Ḥanafiyya, the first upon his departure from Medina and the second upon his departure from Mecca. I believe that this testament is upon his departure from Mecca in the month of Dhū al-Ḥijja. After testifying to the oneness of God ﷻ and the Prophethood of the Prophet ﷺ, the Imām ؑ said, "I did not revolt out of pride or arrogance nor out of a desire to cause corruption or commit tyranny. I only revolted seeking reform in the umma of my grandfather ﷺ."[9] This means that he wanted to revolt for the sake of reform, and not necessarily for attaining either government or martyrdom. Reform is a difficult thing. A person may come into power or he may be martyred in the process. In both cases, the revolt is for the sake of reform. the Imām ؑ continues, "I want to enjoin the good and forbid the evil , and walk in the footsteps of my grandfather."[10] Reform comes from commanding the right and forbidding the wrong; it is a manifestation of this process.

---

[9] Ibid., 329.

[10] Ibid.

When Imām al-Ḥusayn ؑ was in Mecca, he sent two letters. The first was to the notables of Baṣra, and the second was to the notables of Kūfa. In the former, he said, "I sent my messenger to you with this letter, calling you to the book of God and the precept (*sunna*) of his Prophet. The Prophetic sunna has been extinguished and innovation (b*idʿa*) has been restored. If you listen to me, I will guide you to the path of rectitude (*rashād*)." This means that the Imām ؑ was seeking to fulfill the great duty of rejuvenating Islam and the sunna of the Prophet ﷺ.

In his letter to the notables of Kūfa, Imām al-Ḥusayn ؑ explained the reason for his revolt: "By God, the true Imām is but the one who applies the Qurʾān, upholds justice, believes in the Truth, and restrains himself for the sake of God. Peace."[11]

Imām al-Ḥusayn ؑ spoke to the people in all the stations on the way following his departure from Mecca, and he used every method to do so. When he faced the army of al-Ḥurr and the two armies went to opposite sides, Imām al-Ḥusayn ؑ reached the place called al-Bayḍa and said to al-Ḥurr's companions, "O people, the Prophet of God ﷺ said, 'God indeed musters with the tyrannical ruler whoever sees him transgressing the bounds of God, breaking the covenant with God, opposing the sunna of the Prophet of God ﷺ, and

[11] Ibid., 335.

treating the servants of God sinfully and aggressively without bringing about a change through word or deed.'"[12]

The Prophet ﷺ explained what must be done if Islamic order suffers deviation. Imām al-Ḥusayn عليه السلام based himself on this ḥadīth.

In other words, the obligation is this: "bringing about a change through word or deed." If a person was in such a situation and the circumstances were convenient, like we said, he has to revolt no matter what. This is regardless of whether he gets killed, stays alive, appears to succeed, or appears to fail. According to the Prophet ﷺ, every Muslim is obliged to revolt in protest of such a reality.

Imām al-Ḥusayn عليه السلام then said, "I am the most entitled to change things (*anā aḥaqq man ghayyar*). He means he is the most entitled because he is the Prophet's ﷺ grandson. Although the Prophet ﷺ made revolt an obligation upon all Muslims, his grandson, and the inheritor of his knowledge and wisdom, Imām al-Ḥusayn b. ʿAlī عليه السلام is more entitled to revolt. Imām al-Ḥusayn عليه السلام was saying that this was the reason he revolted, announcing that the cause of his revolt is causing a change. He was revolting against corruption.

---

[12] Ibid., 382.

When Imām al-Ḥusayn ﷺ dismounted in Azyad four men joined him, and he said to them, "By God, I hope that whatever God decrees for us will be good, whether we are killed or victorious." This proves my saying that regardless of victory or death, the obligation must be fulfilled.

In his first sermon after dismounting in Karbalā', Imām al-Ḥusayn ﷺ said, "Things with us are as you see ... Don't you see that the truth is not being enforced and falsehood is not being rejected? A faithful person yearns to meet God when he is rightful."

The uprising of Imām al-Ḥusayn ﷺ was to fulfill the obligation of revolting, which is the duty of all Muslims when corruption takes root in Islamic society and threatens to change Islamic rulings as long as the circumstances are right and the revolt was sure to be productive. Remaining alive and not suffering are not necessary conditions for revolt, nor are being free of suffering, torture, and harm.

Imām al-Ḥusayn ﷺ revolted and fulfilled this obligation so that it could be a lesson for everyone. Any person across time could find himself in the right circumstances for revolt. Of course, the circumstances haven't been convenient in the times of the Imāms ﷺ after Imām al-Ḥusayn ﷺ. The reason for this is that other obligations had to be fulfilled then. The proper circumstances haven't been available throughout the times of the Imāms عليهم السلام up to the age of occultation, but they may become available in Islamic countries over time. The conditions may even be available in parts of the Islamic world today. If the Muslims concerned fulfilled this obligation, they will have preserved Islam and guaranteed its survival. People may fail, but when this act of change, revolt, and reform is repeated, rest assured that corruption will be uprooted.

Imām al-Ḥusayn ﵇ contributed a great practical lesson to Islamic history and guaranteed the survival of Islam in his age and in all ages.

Commemorating Imām al-Ḥusayn ﵇ and Karbalāʾ

Wherever there is such corruption, Imām al-Ḥusayn ﵇ will be there to teach us through his example and acts what we need to do. This is why the name of Imām al-Ḥusayn ﵇ and the memory of Karbalāʾ must remain alive; the memory of Karbalāʾ keeps this practical lesson right before us.

Sadly, the lesson of ʿĀshūrāʾ is not as well-known as it should be in other Islamic countries. Nevertheless, in our country, this lesson is well-known; people know Imām al-Ḥusayn ﵇ and the Ḥusaynī spirit is dominant here. For this reason, people were not surprised when Imām Khumaynī قدس سره said that Muḥarram is the month of the victory of blood over the sword. This is a truth; blood indeed triumphed over the sword.

I had mentioned all these points in a mourning ceremony (*majlis*) about twenty-five years before the revolution. I spoke to the brothers and sisters in the audience and asked them how Imām al-Ḥusayn ﷵ showed us what our obligation was.

Imām al-Ḥusayn ﷵ Clarified the Obligation

Those were the circumstances, that was life, and that was the state of Islam. Imām al-Ḥusayn ﷵ had practically explained the responsibility of all generations. Even if none of his words were preserved for us, we would still know our obligation.

A people who are chained and held down by their rulers' corruption and who are controlled by the enemies of the religion must know their obligation. This infallible (*maʿṣūm*) Imām ﷵ and the grandson of the Prophet ﷺ taught us what we have to do. It was impossible for him to do so in words only, for if he said it a thousand times without revolting himself, his call wouldn't have made its mark on history. Advice and sayings don't make history; there are thousands of sayings. Only a great and difficult deed such as the painful sacrifice of Imām al-Ḥusayn ﷵ can have that desired effect.

The truth is that ʿĀshūrāʾ is unique among the calamities of humanity. As Imām ʿAlī ﷵ, the Prophet ﷺ,

and Imām al-Ḥasan ﷺ have said, "There is no day like yours, O Abā ʿAbdillāh."[13]

Distinguishing Primary and Secondary Duties[14]

The Vanguard and the Primary Duty

If the Islamic world and particularly its intellectual look into the dimensions, preliminary conditions, and consequences of ʿĀshūrāʾ, the Islamic way of life and the obligation of Muslim generations in all circumstances becomes clear. One of the most important lessons is that Imām al-Ḥusayn b. ʿAlī ﷺ, at a critical juncture of Islamic history, separated his primary duty (*wājib*) from his other duties and fulfilled that duty. He was not unsure of what Islam needed. This is the weakness that Muslims have always suffered from; the mistake of the vanguard (*al-ṭalīʿa*) and leaders of the umma relates to determining the real duty in a given historical period. They cannot distinguish the most important matter that has to be undertaken, for whose sake other important things must be sacrificed. Movements and deeds are not given their due importance and effort.

---

[13] Ibid., 218.

[14] Sayyid Khāminaʾī's meeting with the scholars and students of the seminary on 7/5/1371 SH.

Deserters of the Real Duty

During Imām al-Ḥusayn's ﷺ time, there were people who would have clung to secondary duties even when they became convinced of the necessity of uprising due to the difficulties and hardships associated with it. Secondary duties became a pretext for some people. Some of those who did not support Imām al-Ḥusayn ﷺ were faithful, pious people. Not all of them were attracted to this world.

At that time, there were symbols and figures in the Islamic world who wanted to fulfill their duty but were not able to discern the obligation, the circumstances of the time, and the real enemy. They confused primary and secondary duties. This itself is a great test for the Islamic world.

The Primary Duty of Society

This is a test that we can face ourselves today, confusing the most important matter with other, less important matters. In such a case, we must search for the primary duty upon which society stands. When the struggle had once revolved around fighting colonialism, despotism, and the regimes of faithless tyrants, some people misdiagnosed the main duty and clung to other deeds. Perhaps they had lessons to offer and publications to issue or perhaps they ran a small seminary that preached the faith (*ḥawza tablīghiyya*). Maybe they were responsible for guiding a small handful of people. They thought that if they entered the fray, they would have to suspend their activities, so they abandoned jihād despite its greatness! This is a mistake in distinguishing the most important duty from lesser duties.

Countering Tyrants

Imām al-Ḥusayn b. ʿAlī عليه السلام made it clear in his speeches for all to hear that the most important duty in those circumstances was fighting tyrannical powers and taking the initiative of saving the umma from their Satanic influence. When Imām al-Ḥusayn عليه السلام went to Iraq to initiate a battle like the battle of Karbalāʾ, it was obvious that he would be deprived of staying in Medina, preaching divine rulings, explaining the teachings of Ahl al-Bayt عليهم السلام, and teaching and educating Muslims. He would no longer be able to instruct people about prayer and relate the ḥadīths of the Prophet ﷺ to them. Naturally, his teachings would be suspended and he would be prevented from preaching knowledge. Similarly, he would no longer be able to help orphans, the needy, and the poor of Medina. All these were duties that the Imām عليه السلام performed before heading to Iraq and that he sacrificed for the sake of his most important duty. As speakers and teachers of Islam relate, he even sacrificed his pilgrimage for the sake of the most important obligation at a time when people were flocking to perform the pilgrimage rites (*manāsik al-ḥajj*). What was this obligation?

Imām al-Ḥusayn b. 'Alī ﷺ Determines the Duty

The obligation, like the Imām ﷺ himself said, was to fight the corrupt ruling regime that was the source of all corruption, as he said, "I want to command the right and forbid the wrong, and walk in the footsteps of my grandfather." This is the obligation. In another sermon on the way to Karbalā', he said, "O people, the Prophet of God ﷺ said, 'God indeed musters with the tyrannical ruler whoever sees him transgressing the bounds of God, breaking the covenant with God... without bringing about a change through word or deed."

The obligation is removing the unjust, tyrannical ruler and his authority that spreads corruption upon the earth and drags humanity to material and spiritual destruction. This is the philosophy behind Imām al-Ḥusayn's ﷺ uprising that is a practical manifestation of commanding the right and forbidding the wrong. These points must be kept in mind when commanding the right and forbidding the wrong. Imām al-Ḥusayn ﷺ acted upon the most important obligation and sacrificed all other obligations for it. He determined the required deed in its right time.

No Place for Confusion

In every age, there is a movement in Islamic society and an enemy threatening Islam and the Muslims; this enemy must be known. If we make a mistake in determining the enemy that is harming and attacking Islam, we will suffer a great, unavoidable loss, and we will lose many opportunities. We have the duty of observing the highest degree of caution, determining the enemies, and knowing the obligations of our people and the Islamic world.

Since the government of Islam has been established and the banner of Islam has been raised in our day, which is unprecedented in Islamic history after the formative period of Islam (*ṣadr al-Islām*), Muslims now have the necessary capabilities. There is no excuse for being oblivious of the enemy and mistaking the side it attacks us from.

Global Arrogance: The Greatest Threat to Islam

From the victory of the Islamic Revolution until today, the entire goal of our great Imām ﷺ and his supporters, regardless of their positions and capabilities, was to determine the biggest danger and greatest threat to the Muslims, the Islamic society in Iran, and the principles of justice and truth in our modern world.

Things are like that today. The greatest attack and the constant danger come from global imperialism and the powers of faithlessness and arrogance. This is the biggest threat to the Muslims. It is true that internal weakness within society paves the way for the enemy to mount its attack. However, this weakness is enforced by the enemy in the first place using various means and tools. We must not fall for this.

Islamic society must go in the opposite direction of the global imperialism and arrogance that control the world today.

The Islamic Awakening Sparked American Animosity

Superpowers oppose Islam and the Islamic awakening (*al-ṣaḥwa al-Islāmiyya*), and they fight Iran because of its adherence to Islam. All their schemes aim to extinguish the Islamic movement in the world. The Global Arrogance, the usurping tyrant, is our foremost enemy, followed by powers great and small that harbor a grudge against Islam because it scares them or harms their interests.

Their animosity to Iran comes from the Islamic awakening that took hold here. Islamic peoples all over the world look up to this movement and this victorious revolution, confidently moving forward. If the enemies succeed in defeating Islam in our spot in the world, God ﷻ forbid, they would achieve their greatest victory over the global Islamic awakening. This is a concrete truth, so we must not make the mistake of misdiagnosing our enemy, and we must not delude ourselves into thinking that the enemy has given up its animosity to Islam and the Muslims.

The Lesson of al-Arbaʿīn: Commemoration and the Reality of Martyrdom[15]

The Importance of al-Arbaʿīn

The Importance of al-Arbaʿīn lies mainly in the fact that the memory of the Ḥusaynī uprising has been forever eternalized on this date due to divine providence and the wisdom of the Prophet ﷺ. Like the Battle of Karbalāʾ, if the families of martyrs and heroes waver in upholding the memory of their beloved martyrs, future generations will not be able to enjoy the fruits of martyrdom.

It's true that God ﷻ took it upon Himself to resurrect martyrs in the Hereafter and that a martyr lives on in people's memories throughout history, but God ﷻ created a material cause for the memorialization of martyrs that depends on our will and choices. We are the ones who can commemorate our martyrs and the cause and philosophy of martyrdom by making the right decision.

ʿĀshūrāʾ Lives on Forever

Sayyidah Zaynab al-Kubrā ؑ and Imām al-Sajjād ؑ engaged in their jihad and revealed the truth of ʿĀshūrāʾ and the goal of Imām al-Ḥusayn b. ʿAlī ؑ in his uprising

---

[15] *Ḥadīth al-Wilāya*, Vol. 2, p. 141-143.

against injustice throughout their days of captivity, whether on the afternoon of ʿĀshūrāʾ, on the way to Kūfa and Shām, in Shām itself, or back in Karbalāʾ on their way to Medina. They continued these efforts throughout their lives. Had they not done so, ʿĀshūrāʾ wouldn't have remained alive, active, and glowing until our day.

Why did Imām Jaʿfar al-Ṣādiq ﵇ say, "Whoever recites poetry about al-Ḥusayn and cries and causes other people to cry will be granted Paradise and God's forgiveness"?[16] It was because entire media apparatuses were dedicated to isolating and obscuring the cause of ʿĀshūrāʾ and Ahl al-Bayt ﵇ in order to keep the umma ignorant of what really happened. This is what preaching (tablīgh) is all about. Then as now, the powers of injustice were making the most of fake and biased news.

Can such a great incident that happened in an isolated desert preserve its vitality and power in such circumstances? Undoubtedly, its fate would have been oblivion without the previously-mentioned efforts.

This incident was preserved thanks to the efforts of Imām al-Ḥusayn b. ʿAlī's ﵇ family. They faced obstacles, and it was very difficult. It was as difficult as

[16] al-Majlisī, al-ʿAllamah Muḥammad Bāqir, *Biḥār al-Anwār*, Vol. 44, p. 283.

Imām al-Ḥusayn b. ʿAlī's ﷺ jihād. This is how difficult the jihād of Sayyidah Zaynab al-Kubrā ﷺ, Imām al-Sajjād ﷺ, and the rest of the pure ones ﷺ was. Their arena was not military but that of media and culture; we must pay attention to that.

The Lesson of al-Arbaʿīn

The lesson that the day of al-Arbaʿīn teaches us is the necessity of commemorating martyrdom and upholding its truth in the face of the enemy's media. You've noticed the magnitude of anti-revolution media that opposed Imām Khumaynī ﷺ, Islam, and our people from the victory of the revolution until today.

The media was dedicated to fighting us as we defended Islam, our homeland, and the dignity and honor of our people. Notice the direct and indirect practices of the enemy against our dear martyrs who sacrificed their most precious belongings, i.e. their souls, for the sake of God ﷻ. The enemy did this using channels, newspapers, magazines, books, and lectures that it's been using to fill the heads of simple people around the world.

This handful of naïve and ignorant persons in our country, both famous and unknown, have gone to the extent of saying ignorant and erroneous things right in the middle of this intense war. This caused great pain to our dear Imām Khumaynī ﷺ and made him call out and reveal divine truths frankly. If the enemy media had not been faced with truthful media, and if the Iranian people, with its speakers, authors, artists, did not dedicate itself to serving the truth, the enemy would have triumphed in the arena of the media. This arena is very great and dangerous.

Of course, the majority of our people are immune to enemy media. That is only due to the blessing that is consciousness that arose after the revolution. The enemy's lies and its reversal of the truths that our people see with their own eyes made our umma lose its confidence as it witnessed the enemy's statements and schemes and the noise of the global media.

Yazīd's tyrannical media apparatus tried to condemn Imām al-Ḥusayn b. ʿAlī ؏ and portray him as a rebel who revolted against just Islamic rule for his own worldly desires! Some believed this false news. When Imām al-Ḥusayn ؏ was shockingly and painfully martyred at the hands of the unjust on the soil of Karbalāʾ, his killing was portrayed as an amazing victory! However, the righteous media apparatus of the Imāmate reversed all these schemes; this is what the Truth really is.

The Philosophy of the Uprising of ʿĀshūrāʾ[17]

Rescuing the Umma From Ignorance

In one of the visitation formulas that are addressed to Imām al-Ḥusayn ﷺ on the Day of al-Arbaʿīn, there is a very touching phrase. It is this: "... and sacrificed his soul for Your sake in order to save your servants from ignorance (*jahāla*) and the perplexity of error (*ḍalāla*)." Imām al-Ḥusayn's ﷺ philosophy of sacrifice is summarized in this phrase. Contemplate its sophisticated and lofty meaning.

Who Can Save Humanity?

Humanity is constantly threatened by the devils' schemes. Devils, great and small, have made it their habit to sacrifice whole nations and peoples to achieve their goals. You're familiar with history; you know how unjust and tyrannical rulers have dealt with nations. You're witnessing our modern world and how superpowers are aiming to subject people to the temptations and tricks of the devils. God's ﷻ servants need help to save themselves from ignorance, error, and deviation.

Who can save humanity? Those who are seized by greed, whims, and desires cannot save anyone because they are

[17] *Ḥadīth al-Wilāya*, Vol. 5, p. 147-148.

in error themselves, nor can those who are seized by selfishness and wishful thinking. A person who can save them must appear, or else divine grace (*lutf*) might include them and inspire them to save themselves. A person who can save humanity has to be selfless, for he has to make sacrifices and abandon desires, wishful thinking, love of oneself, selfishness, greed, whims, envy, stinginess, and all the other chains that bind humanity. This savior can then light the candle that will illuminate humanity's path to freedom.

The Eternal Sun of 'Āshūrā'[18]

'Āshūrā''s Blessings

Despite all that has been said about the benefits of Muḥarram and 'Āshūrā' and their consequences, the more time passes, the brighter this eternal sun shines. It is the sun of martyrdom, suffering injustice, and the estrangement of jihād (*ghurbat al-jihād*), a sun that blazed thanks to Imām al-Ḥusayn b. 'Alī ﷺ and his companions. The blessings of 'Āshūrā' became more known day after day. From the first day of 'Āshūrā', its deep, fundamental consequences began to gradually emerge. Some people knew their obligation at that time; the movement of the penitents (*al-tawwābūn*) emerged

[18] Sayyid Khāmina'ī's meeting with the scholars and students of the seminary as well as preachers and speakers on the eve of Muḥarram of the year 1416 AH.

and the Hashemites and sons of Imām al-Ḥusayn عليه السلام engaged in lengthy jihād. Even the Abbasid revolution began in the name of Imām al-Ḥusayn b. ʿAlī عليه السلام. The Abbasids revolted against the Umayyads in the mid-second Hijri century and sent their missionaries (*duʿāt*) to the Islamic world, and particularly to the eastern regions of Persia, such as Khurāsān, paving the way for the fall of the tyrannical, arrogant, and racist Umayyad rule. If you read historical works, you will realize that when the Abbasid missionaries spread everywhere in the Islamic world, they made the blood of Imām al-Ḥusayn b. ʿAlī عليه السلام and his martyrdom a rallying cry for their revolution. They made their slogan vengeance for the Prophet's ﷺ grandson and the beloved of al-Zahrāʾ عليها السلام in an attempt to make their propaganda succeed.

People responded sympathetically to the Abbasids. Even the black color that they took for themselves over five hundred years of rule had been chosen in mourning of Imām al-Ḥusayn عليه السلام. They used to say, "This is the mourning of Muḥammad's family." This is how the Abbasids began their revolution and caused a change. However, they deviated and behaved like the Umayyads later.

This was one of ʿĀshūrāʾ's consequences, and there were many such consequences across history. The circumstances of our age—the dominance of injustice, faithlessness, and atheism, when justice came to mean breaking the law and tyranny became the law ruling the globe—are a manifest consequence of 'Āshūrā'.

Imām Khumaynī and the Inspiration of 'Āshūrā'

The arrogance of the superpowers that are trying to establish a new world order that dominates the world is injustice itself. They give tyranny, injustice, and racism lawful names, pretending they are human rights. This is the worst kind of injustice since tyranny is disguising itself as fairness and injustice is disguising itself as justice. During such a difficult time, the veils of darkness were removed, the sun of truth shone bright, and justice came to rule. Islam declared its presence although everyone was seeking to exclude it, and it forced the world to accept authentic Islam as a world order. This was one of 'Āshūrā''s blessings, just as the beginning of the Islamic Revolution was one of 'Āshūrā''s blessings.

Our great Imām drew inspiration from Muḥarram and the Battle of 'Āshūrā' and made the call of the truth come out of his heart and reach the umma and change it. Our past martyrs in Tehran and Ramin and other places were participants in the mourning ceremonies (*'azā'*) of Imām al-Ḥusayn. The vanguard of martyrs of the 15 Khordad uprising were attacked by the enemies of 'Āshūrā'. You saw how our great Imām drew inspiration and lessons from Muḥarram in the year 1357 (1978), proposing the concept of "the victory of blood over the sword," and achieved his goal. By following Imām al-Ḥusayn ﷺ, the Iranian people drew lessons from 'Āshūrā' and blood triumphed over the sword.

We are the Guardians of 'Āshūrā'

Today, we are the inheritors and guardians of this historical truth. Those who want to know what happened on the tenth of Muḥarram to learn from it and commemorate it want to hear it from the scholars and male and female preachers (*muballighūn*, sing *muballigh*). Here emerges the issue of preaching, which is very important. The young students and the esteemed persons in the seminary, as well as preachers, speakers, and panegyrists have used the incident of 'Āshūrā' to face the darkness that is dominating humanity, tearing away the veils of evil using this divine weapon, and displaying the sun of truth through the rulership (*ḥākimiyya*) of Islam. This is a truth and a miracle that has been witnessed in our own age. Why don't we expect scholars, preachers, and speakers everywhere and at all times to raise the sword of the truth and the blade of Imām 'Alī's ﷺ Dhū l-Fiqār in the face of all falsehood? Why do we think this is improbable now even though the enemy's media had been stronger in that period and the darkness was denser? It's true that enemy media in our age has dominated the intellectual domain of humanity and vast sums have been dedicated to distort the image of Islam and Shī'ism. Anyone who has unlawful interests in the lives of peoples and their countries sees himself obligated to work against Islam and Islamic rule. This means that faithlessness is divided upon itself, but all of its elements have agreed on fighting authentic Islam. They have even pitted false Islam against authentic Islam.

This is all true, but despite the malicious enemy media, can't the truth and authentic Islam recreate that miracle thanks to the blessing of ‘Āshūrā’ and the message of Muḥarram? It's not easy, but it is possible; it requires effort and sacrifice, and it is our responsibility.

Our world today is hungry for the truth. This is not the talk of an Islamic scholar or a Muslim extremist. It is the talk of people who have been in touch with Western culture for years, and who look fondly upon the West and its theorists. These people are saying that the most important segment of Western society is hungry for Islam.

The Problems of Modern Western Urban Life

The most important segment includes scholars, intellectuals, conscientious individuals, cultured people, and the youth. They are the most important elements in the edifice of Western society, and they are eager for a school or a lesson that can save them from the thousands of real problems of everyday life. Many problems in life aren't actually real; a real problem would be the loss of spiritual safety, feelings of estrangement, depression, instability, and the lack of peace and serenity. These are the real problems of human life, such as when a person finds himself forced to commit suicide at the height of his fame and fortune. Why would a young rich person with the means of enjoying life kill himself? Is there a pain greater than the absence of money and the lack of physical and sexual pleasure?

Losing peace and serenity, the lack of a spiritual center, the absence of companionship and connection among people, and the feeling of estrangement and brokenness are all pains that modern Western urban life suffers from, and sensitive segments of society feel these pains more keenly. This is why such people await someone to rid them of these pains. In any place where the level of awareness is high, people look to Islam to be saved. Although some people lack the awareness and do not even know of Islam, the circumstances are favorable for the adoption of Islam. As for those who already know Islam, they seek refuge only in Islam.

An Iranian intellectual who recently passed away had said that the West today is looking for figures such as Shaykh al-Anṣārī and Mullā Ṣadrā. The lives, morals, and values of these two men have attracted Western figures and intellectuals.

Knowing ʿĀshūrāʾ is the Pinnacle of Islamic Knowledge

The fountain of values was here, and the pinnacle of knowledge was the knowledge of ʿĀshūrāʾ. We must understand the value of this matter since we want to present this knowledge to the world. In this regard, I can only thank those who responded to my call last year and purified the ceremonies of ʿĀshūrāʾ from distortion.

Countering the Distortion of ʿĀshūrāʾ

Dear believers in Imām al-Ḥusayn b. ʿAlī ﵇, I want to stress this again. Imām al-Ḥusayn b. ʿAlī ﵇ can save the world today as long as his image is not distorted. Don't allow incorrect concepts and distortions to distract the eyes and the hearts away from the Master of Martyrs ﵇. We must stand up to distortion. I will summarize my point in a few words. First, we must continue to uphold the cause of Imām al-Ḥusayn b. ʿAlī ﵇ on the pulpits and through traditional eulogies, highlighting the incidents of the eve and the day of ʿĀshūrāʾ. After all, time erases even major incidents. But the incident of ʿĀshūrāʾ is eternal down to its last details due to the blessing of these commemorative gatherings. Of course, the truth must be revealed in an expert way as presented in Ibn Ṭawūs's *al-Luhūf* and al-Mufīd's *al-Irshād*.

Clarifying Imām al-Ḥusayn's ﷺ Goals

Therefore, we must recount the events, read eulogies (*rithāʾ*) and panegyrics (*madīḥ*), beat our chests, and explain the incident of ʿĀshūrāʾ and the goals of Imām al-Ḥusayn ﷺ through enriching lectures that recount his sayings. Examples of these sayings are: "I did not revolt out of pride or arrogance nor out of a desire to cause corruption or commit tyranny. I but revolved seeking reform in the umma of my grandfather," and "O people, the Prophet of God said, 'God indeed musters with the tyrannical ruler whoever sees him transgressing the bounds of God, breaking the covenant with God, opposing the sunna of the Prophet of God , and treating the servants of God sinfully and aggressively without bringing about a change through word or deed.'" These are the best of lessons. Another example is Imām al-Ḥusayn's ﷺ saying, "Let anyone who is willing to sacrifice his soul for our sake and prepare himself for meeting his Lord depart with us." The talk here is about meeting God ﷻ, which is the purpose of creation. God ﷻ has said, "O man! You are laboring toward your Lord laboriously, and you will encounter Him."[19] All this striving and hardship is but for this purpose: "You will encounter Him." Anyone who has prepared himself for meeting God ﷻ was to leave with Imām al-Ḥusayn ﷺ. It was unlawful for such a person to stay at home, cling to this world, and turn a

---

[19] Sūrat al-Inshiqāq, Verse 6.

blind eye to Imām al-Ḥusayn ﷺ. We have to move, and this movement begins with disciplining the self and then targeting society and the world at large. These are the goals and conclusions of Imām al-Ḥusayn ﷺ's revolt.

The Actions of a Ḥusaynī, Karbalā'ī Person

The essence of Imām al-Ḥusayn's ﷺ revolt lies in the fact that the Imām ﷺ witnessed a time when the world was in the grip of injustice and tyranny, and no one had the courage to speak the truth. The darkness was so heavy that even 'Abdullāh b. Ja'far and 'Abdullāh b. 'Abbās did not depart with Imām al-Ḥusayn ﷺ. What does that mean? Doesn't it indicate the state the world was in back then?

Imām al-Ḥusayn ﷺ stood alone to face injustice in those circumstances with a handful of people alongside him; he would have stood up even if that handful wasn't present. Let us suppose that when Imām al-Ḥusayn ﷺ said to his companions on the eve of 'Āshūrā', "You are not accountable if you leave me," they all left, including al-'Abbās and 'Alī al-Akbār. What would have happened then? Would the Imām ﷺ have backed down or would he have remained steadfast and fought? In our own age, there came a man who said, "Even if I remained alone and the whole world conspired against me, I will not back down." That was our Imām ﷺ; he committed to his word and was truthful, so he became an exemplar of "men who fulfill what they have pledged to God."[20] Do you see now what a man who was raised up in the school of ʿĀshūrāʾ and Imām al-Ḥusayn ﷺ is able to do? If we were all raised up in the school of ʿĀshūrāʾ, the whole world would have hastened toward reform and prepared itself for the appearance of the ultimate master of truth, Imām al-Mahdī ﷺ.

These concepts must be explained to the umma in mourning ceremonies that contain sermons, lamentations, and praise. Preachers have to speak in all sorts of ways to the people in villages and cities all over the country and all over the world from behind their pulpits and podiums about the goal of Imām al-Ḥusayn ﷺ. The speaker might include a moral lesson or a speech on local or global politics; that is fine. However, his speech has to relate to ʿĀshūrāʾ either explicitly or implicitly, and either separately or as part of the larger lecture so that ʿĀshūrāʾ doesn't remain unknown or covered up.

Revealing the Truths of Islam During Muḥarram

Secondly, we must benefit from this chance to do what Imām al-Ḥusayn ﷺ did when he rejuvenated Islam using the blessing of his jihād. Islam renewed its liveliness and won its freedom thanks to the revolt and blood of Imām al-Ḥusayn b. ʿAlī ﷺ.

[20] Sūrat al-Ahzāb, Verse 23.

Drawing inspiration from the memory, name, and pulpit of Imām al-Ḥusayn ﷺ, you have to reveal the truths of Islam, let people know about the Qur'ān and the Prophetic sunna, and explain *Nahj al-Balāgha* to them. Among Islamic truths there is a blessed truth that became manifest in Iran; this truth is the Islamic Republic, the order of the Prophet ﷺ, 'Alī ﷺ, and wilāya. The government of truth is of the loftiest components of Islamic knowledge. Let no one imagine that the truths of Islam can be revealed without the rulership of Islam that manifested itself today in this country.

Sacrificing to Preserve Islam[21]

Insight is Necessary When Defending Religion

'Āshūrā' contains lessons; the most important lesson is preserving religion. Everything must be sacrificed for the Qur'ān's sake. Everyone, young and old, men and women, the noble and the humble, and the Imām and his subjects, must all stand together in support of the truth and against falsehood. The front of falsehood is apparently empowered but in truth it couldn't be weaker. It is similar to the front of the Umayyads, which was shattered at the hands of the caravan of the captives in Kūfa, Shām, and Medina until the family of Abū

[21] Sayyid Khāmina'ī's meeting with commanders and members of the 'Āshūrā' Brigade on 22/4/1371 AH.

Sufyān was forgotten. The lesson here is that insight is the most important thing when defending religion. Those who lack insight are quickly deceived and lured to the side of falsehood without even realizing it. Some of those who supported Ibn Ziyād were neither profligate (*fussāq*, sing. *fāsiq*) nor immoral (*fujjār*, sing *fājir*); they only lacked insight.

These are the lessons of ʿĀshūrāʾ, and they are enough to raise an entire umma from a state of humiliation to a state of might and to defeat the fronts of faithlessness and arrogance. They are lessons that make up life.

The Uprightness of Imām al-Ḥusayn عليه السلام and Imām Khumaynī قدس سره [22]

There are two kinds of victory. The first is the victory a person witnesses himself; establishing a government and defeating the enemies of the revolution was like that, as the Imām قدس سره saw his victory with his own eyes. The second kind of victory, and it is the more important of the two, is the victory across eternity. This is the victory of thought and method; it is the victory of the prophets despite all the hardships of their lives. This is an intellectual and methodological victory that a great and intelligent person is able to achieve. The Imām قدس سره achieved this second victory as well. This is the goal of

---

[22] *Jombhūrī Islamī,* 16/3/1375 SH.

commemorating this great man at this annual celebration every year.

The Similarities Between Imām al-Ḥusayn عليه السلام and Imām Khumaynī قدس سره

Here I would like to discuss something about the movement of our great Imām قدس سره that is a lesson to us. I call upon people who know about thought, politics, and important causes to contemplate this issue and delve deeper into it.

You know that there are many similarities between the movement of Imām Khumaynī قدس سره and the movement of Imām al-Ḥusayn عليه السلام. The movement of Imām Khumaynī قدس سره even sprang out of the Ḥusaynī uprising. Although the original movement, that of Imām al-Ḥusayn عليه السلام, ended in the martyrdom of all its members and the movement Imām Khumaynī قدس سره ended in victory, this is not a substantial difference. Both movements had similar motives, circumstances, and plans. The only difference between them was in the outcomes; the former movement ended in the martyrdom of Imām al-Ḥusayn عليه السلام while the latter movement ended in our great Imām قدس سره establishing a government. This is something that is generally clear.

Uprightness in the Face of Difficulties

A prominent common element between the two movements is uprightness (*istiqāma*). We must not brush aside the issue of uprightness so quickly, as it is very important. The uprightness of Imām al-Ḥusayn ﵇ made him decide not to surrender to Yazīd and his tyrannical rule. This was when the struggle began; Imām al-Ḥusayn ﵇ refused to surrender to the rule of a corrupt person who strove to distort Islam beyond recognition. When Imām al-Ḥusayn ﵇ set out from Medina, he had this intention in mind. As he reached Mecca and felt that there were enough people supporting him, he turned his movement into a revolution. The essence of the matter in all cases is an objection to a government that was unacceptable to Imām al-Ḥusayn ﵇ on all accounts. At the beginning, Imām al-Ḥusayn ﵇ stood up to this government when matters were still uncertain but he did not make his objections known. Soon, Imām al-Ḥusayn ﵇ faced problem after problem, beginning with being forced to leave Mecca and ending in fighting in Karbalā' and its hardships.

Legitimate Excuses Hold People Back

Legitimate excuses can stop a person from performing mighty deeds. Perhaps a person may have a duty or obligation, but when the time comes to perform it an important obstacle comes up, such as the death of a large number of people. In that case, that person might think he is no longer obligated to do his duty.

Notice the number of legitimate excuses that sprang up before Imām al-Ḥusayn ﵇ and had the potential of deterring a superficial person from his goal. These excuses include the abandonment of Muslim b. ʿAqīl by the people of Kūfa, which resulted in his death. Imām al-Ḥusayn ﵇ could have said that he now had a legitimate excuse and that he was no longer obligated to go through with his plans. He could have said that they had not wanted to pledge allegiance to Yazīd but it became clear that it was difficult to do so in such circumstances that the people could not withstand. Imām al-Ḥusayn ﵇ could have said that he was forced to pledge allegiance as his obligation was no longer valid.

The second legitimate excuse arose in Karbalāʾ itself. Imām al-Ḥusayn ﵇ could have appealed to logic by saying, "These women and children cannot withstand this burning desert, so my obligation is no longer valid." In such a case, he would have had to surrender and accept all the things that he had formerly refused. Another legitimate excuse concerns the tenth day of Muḥarram when the battle began and many of the Imām's ﵇ companions were martyred. At that point, Imām al-Ḥusayn ﵇ was facing many hardships and he could have said that it was now clear that one could do nothing to oppose these people, so he had to retreat. A new legitimate excuse came up when the Imām ﵇

became certain that he would be martyred and that the womenfolk of the Prophet ﷺ and Imām ʿAlī ؑ would be held captive by strangers in that vast desert. Here the issue of honor comes in. Imām al-Ḥusayn ؑ, being an honorable person, could have said, "My obligation is suspended now that it means my death and the capture of the daughters of the Prophet ﷺ and Imām ʿAlī ؑ, who are the purest women in all of Islam, at the hands of enemies who do not know the meaning of honor."

Brothers and sisters, think deeply about this. It is a matter worthy of attention: if Imām al-Ḥusayn ؑ wanted to consider the horrifying incidents that were coming — such as the death of ʿAlī al-Aṣghar, the captivity of the women, the thirst of the children, and the death of his robust sons—through the eyes of a man of the law and forget his mission, he could have surrendered from the start and pledged allegiance to Yazīd because "necessities make the prohibited permissible (*al-ḍarūrāt tubīḥ al-maḥẓūrāt*)." He did not do so, however. This is what Ḥusaynī uprightness is all about.

Uprightness in the Face of Legitimate Excuses

Uprightness doesn't always mean bearing hardships, as bearing hardships is a lot easier for a great person than bearing matters that seem to be against the Sharia, common custom (*ʿurf*, pl. *aʿrāf*), and plain reason.

A person may be told not to go somewhere to avoid getting tortured or killed or to avoid the death of other people. He may be told that a number of men, women, and children would be harmed due to his insistence. This person may refuse to stop and welcome death and other consequences. Even those who are not afraid of death may slip. Those who never slip possess insight and knowledge about the importance of their actions as well as personal strength. Imām al-Ḥusayn ﷺ displayed both characteristics in Karbalā' so Karbalā' shone like the sun over history, and so it will always remain.

Imām Khumaynī ﵀ on Imām al-Ḥusayn's ﷺ Path

Our great Imām ﵀ walked in the footsteps of Imām al-Ḥusayn ﷺ, leading the revolution to victory, and guaranteed the persistence of this victory after his passing. The manifestation of the victory of his thought and path is your great gathering here and the attraction of people to Islam and the Imām ﵀ at the global level. These victories only came about because of the Imām's ﵀ uprightness.

The Imām ﵀ was told one day that if he were to continue his movement, he would suspend the activities of the Qom seminary. Imām Khumaynī ﵀ was unwavering and moved forward. He was told that major scholars and marāji would move against him and disagreements would tear the Islamic world apart. Although many people would be seized by fear in such a case, Imām Khumaynī قدس سره was unshaken and he committed to his path until the victory of the revolution.

Imām Khumaynī قدس سره was asked countless times, "You are urging the Iranian people to face the Pahlavi Regime, so who will be responsible for the blood that will be spilled?" In other words, they confronted him with the blood of the youth. In the year 1342 SH (1963 AD) or 1344 SH (1965 AD), a great scholar asked me, "If Imām Khumaynī قدس سره went through with the 15 Khordad uprising, and our best youth were killed, who would be responsible for their blood?"

This was how people were thinking. Such thinking causes pressure and can make any person change his mind and not continue with his movement. Imām Khumaynī قدس سره took refuge in his uprightness, however, which shows the greatness of his spirit and insight.

All of that was during the period of jihād against the tyrannical Pahlavi regime. The period that came after that is a lesson to us, and I called on intellectuals, political theorists, and analysts to focus on it. This is a very important stage. Back then jihād was only against the Pahlavi regime, but as soon as the Islamic Republic was established, the arena of conflict expanded and its means changed, and the enemies began their struggle against the Islamic Republic.

These enemies are the authoritarian powers and the global arrogance that are dominating people. These powers harbor animosity toward the Islamic Republic because it threatens their interests and schemes of expansion. The existence of the Islamic Republic amid other Islamic countries threatens the authoritarian powers' dominance over these countries. In other words, if instead of Imām Khumaynī ﷺ we had a weak man, the procession would have stopped due to the presence of excuses and obstacles. Such a man would have retreated and claimed that he was unable to stand up to global arrogance. Imām Khumaynī ﷺ, however, did not do this.

Imām Khumaynī's ﷺ Uprightness in the Face of Enemy Attacks

To realize the importance of this issue, contemplate what I am about to say. Iran was subjected to a multi-level, comprehensive political attack by the media. Political attacks are often effective. We notice this today because the media, whether the television or the radio, terrifies governments due to its effect on peoples. Such a comprehensive attack was mounted against the regime of the Islamic Republic. Of course, our people were insightful, steadfast, and unwavering, and Imām Khumaynī ﷺ did not retreat although all those sides were conspiring against our country. Imām Khumaynī ﷺ didn't say, “We may be able to defeat America on its own, but how are we to defeat both America and the

Soviet Union?" The world was dominated by two poles, and they were both united against us. Imām Khumaynī قدس سره took refuge in his rectitude and held fast to his slogans and path. Never once did he utter something that might please the enemies. It is a Ḥusaynī uprightness; based on the standards of our age, it is a stance equivalent to Imām al-Ḥusayn's stance.

When the war that was enforced on Iran began, our country inherited the disrepair it suffered during the tyrannical Pahlavi regime. It needed reconstruction, but the enemy attacked us unawares, destroying railways and oil refineries. This suspended the work of the petroleum industry and locomotive manufacturers. Any country would have collapsed in such a situation. Everyone knows that the Iraqi regime was not our only opponent; there were also the Soviet Union, France, NATO, American experts, and others. Had Imām Khumaynī قدس سره been weak, he would have claimed that his obligation was lifted and he would have backed down from adhering to Islamic rulings and combatting Israel. This was what they wanted and what they were pushing for, but the Imām قدس سره remained steadfast and did not hesitate. When he agreed to the ceasefire, it wasn't because of enemy pressures but because of the economic problems that the experts told the Imām قدس سره about. These economic experts told the Imām قدس سره that the country was unable to withstand the war with such a budget, so the Imām قدس سره had to accept the international resolution. His acceptance, however, wasn't out of fear:

he didn't worry about being attacked or heed America's threats that it would involve itself in the war directly. After all, America was already intervening. Even if the whole world came to join the war, Imām Khumaynī ﷺ was not the type of person to back down before threats.

Enemy Pressures on Imām Khumaynī ﷺ

Imām Khumaynī ﷺ never happened to hesitate throughout the ten years he spent following the victory of the Islamic Revolution, neither due to the heavy responsibility on his shoulders nor due to enemy threats. This means that Imām Khumaynī ﷺ had a Ḥusaynī spirit. Any war involves losses, and the Imām ﷺ took pride in his people. He felt their pain and sometimes cried on their behalf, tears welling in his eyes. This is something that we witnessed countless times. He's a merciful and kind person with a heart overflowing with love and humanity, but he was not shaken by threats and did not abandon his path. Throughout those ten years, all the enemies of the revolution realized that the Imām ﷺ could not be intimidated despite their efforts. This is a great blessing; the enemy knew that it was impossible to force this man out of the political arena by fear and intimidation. With his shining spirit and personality, Imām Khumaynī ﷺ acted in a way that made the whole world understand that he could not be excluded from the scene neither by pressures and threats nor by turning those threats into actions. They had to accept the reality of the revolution.

We can summarize all that was said in two points. Of course, this summary itself could be expanded and contemplated.

The first point is that one of the manifest phenomena of the 'Āshūrā' uprising is the uprightness of Imām al-Ḥusayn عليه السلام.

The second point is that our great Imām Khumaynī قدس سره modeled his uprising, movement, and life after the Ḥusaynī path. This is why he succeeded in preserving the Islamic Republic and in forcing the enemy to give up its threats and pressures by making it understand that threats and pressures were uselessness and that he قدس سره was not the type of person to back down.

Contemplating the Morals of ʿĀshūrāʾ

Killing the Prophet ﷺ's Son[23]

Contemplating the Reign of Islam

Three main points come up when discussing ʿĀshūrāʾ. They are:

1. Studying the causes and motives behind Imām al-Ḥusayn's ؑ revolt and analyzing it religiously, scientifically, and politically. I have already spoken in detail about this issue, and there are valuable studies by great and virtuous scholars. This is why I will not be discussing this issue today.

2. Discussing the lessons inspired by ʿĀshūrāʾ. This is a lively and everlasting discussion that is not limited to a specific time. The lessons of ʿĀshūrāʾ are sacrifice, ransom, piety, courage, solace, rising up for the sake of God ﷻ, loving Him, and melting in Him. The great revolution that the great Iranian people brought about by rallying around the Imām al-Ḥusayn ؑ of your time and the grandson of Abū ʿAbdillāh ؑ is one of the lessons of ʿĀshūrāʾ. I'm not going to discuss these lessons today either.

---

[23] Sayyid Khāminaʾī's Friday prayer sermon on 18/2/1377 SH.

3. Contemplating the morals (*'ibar*, sing. *'ibra)* of 'Āshūrā'. I spoke about this topic a few years back when I pointed out that 'Āshūrā' contains lessons and morals as well. Discussing 'Āshūrā' concerns the time of the rulership of Islam. In other words, we can say that this discussion concerns the time in which we are living. We have to reflect on the moral behind this.

I made my point in the following way. What happened to that Islamic society that rallied around the Prophet ﷺ, loved him deeply, and firmly believed in him? It was a vibrant and religiously devoted society that grew strong in light of the rulings that we will speak of later. Some people had been alive during the time of the Prophet ﷺ, but they conspired to kill the Prophet's Grandson (a), a most gruesome death. Are there worse examples of apostasy, regression, and deviation?

Sayyidah Zaynab al-Kubrā (a) gave an eloquent sermon in the market of Kūfa about this. She said, "O people of Kūfa, you people of treason and treachery. Do you cry?" This was because when they saw Imām al-Ḥusayn's (a) head on a spear and the daughter of 'Alī (a) held captive, they realized the extent of the tragedy and cried. Sayyidah Zaynab al-Kubrā (a) told them, "May your tears never stop and may your moans never cease. You are like her who would undo her yarn, breaking it up after [spinning it to] strength by making your oaths a means of [mutual] deceit among yourselves."[24]

This is the very meaning of apostasy and regression. Sayyidah Zaynab al-Kubrā ؑ was saying that they were actually like the woman who spun her yarn and then undid it all. She told the Kūfans that they undid their yarn, which is regression itself. This is the moral of the incident, and every Islamic society is susceptible to such a danger.

The height of honor for Imām Khumaynī ؒ was that he motivated the umma to follow the ḥadīths of the Prophet ﷺ. Can people who aren't prophets and infallibles even be compared to the Prophet ﷺ who built up that society?

And yet that same society committed the crime of killing Imām al-Ḥusayn ؑ, which begs the question: is every Islamic society susceptible to such a fate?

If society contemplates the situation, it will not suffer a similar fate, but if it forgoes contemplation it could sink to such depths. This is why the morals behind ʿĀshūrāʾ are important.

We have been, thanks be to God ﷻ and His grace, guided to following this path again, reviving Islam in

[24] Sūrat al-Naḥl, Verse 92.

the world, and raising the banner of the Qurʾān. The Iranian people, whose revolution happened almost twenty years ago, achieved this merit, and they have persisted on this path. However, if we become oblivious and do not be careful, we might suffer the same fate. This is the moral of ʿĀshūrāʾ.

Now I would like to talk about an issue that I raised a few years ago. I noticed that the virtuous scholars have discussed it and written about it extensively, thanks be to God ﷻ. Of course, the time allotted for the Friday sermon is not enough to expand on this issue, as it is an elaborate topic. However, I will discuss it in detail on other occasions if God ﷻ willed it and helped me to do so.

The Greatness of Karbalāʾ

First and foremost, we must realize the gravity of the incident of Karbalāʾ. After that, we can move on to tracing its causes. Let no one think that ʿĀshūrāʾ was only a massacre in which a number of people were killed. No. During ʿĀshūrāʾ, as we read in the visitation (*ziyāra*) of ʿĀshūrāʾ: "great was the calamity and heavy and great was the disaster." To explain just how great this catastrophe was, I will briefly outline three periods of Imām al-Ḥusayn's ؑ life so that we may see his character during these periods. Could someone imagine that crowds of people belonging to his grandfather's ﷺ umma would besiege him, kill him and his companions and menfolk a most gruesome death, and take his dependents captive?

These three periods are:

1. The period of childhood, which began from his earliest days to the death of the Prophet ﷺ.

2. The period of his youth, spanning twenty-five years, from the death of his grandfather ﷺ to the caliphate of the Commander of the Believers ؑ.

3. The period from the martyrdom of Imām 'Alī ؑ to the incident of Karbalā', spanning twenty years.

Imām al-Ḥusayn ؑ as a Child

During the first period, or in the reign of the Prophet ﷺ, Imām al-Ḥusayn ؑ was a child who the Prophet ﷺ loved and doted upon. The Prophet ﷺ had a daughter ؑ, and all the Muslims knew that he had said, "What angers Fāṭimah ؑ angers me and what pleases her pleases me." Look at the great status of this daughter ؑ to be honored with such words for all the Muslims and the world to hear. This is not a trivial thing.

The noble Prophet ﷺ married his daughter ؑ to a person who was at the peak of virtue, i.e. Imām 'Alī b. Abī Ṭālib ؑ. He was a brave, honorable young man who was the most faithful and the first to embrace

Islam. Islam stood upon the sword of Imām ʿAlī ﵇ who always went forward when others held back and who resolved complicated problems. This beloved and dear son-in-law was not loved simply because of family ties. The Prophet ﷺ loved him for the loftiness of his character, which was why he gave ʿAlī ﵇ his daughter ﵇'s hand in marriage. Their marriage resulted in Imām al-Ḥusayn ﵇, and of course Imām al-Ḥasan ﵇ too, but my talk today revolves around Imām al-Ḥusayn ﵇. Imām al-Ḥusayn ﵇ was the dearest beloved of the Prophet ﷺ, and Prophet ﷺ was the leader of the Islamic world, the ruler of the Muslims, and the beloved of all. Prophet Muḥammad ﷺ used to hug Imām al-Ḥusayn ﵇ and take him along to the mosque. The Muslims knew that this child is the Prophet's ﷺ beloved, and they all loved the Prophet ﷺ. Once, when the Prophet ﷺ was giving a sermon from his pulpit, this child tripped and fell. The Prophet ﷺ made sure to go down from his pulpit to hug and console him. This was how much the Prophet ﷺ loved Imām al-Ḥusayn ﵇.

When Imām al-Ḥasan and Imām al-Ḥusayn ﵇ were six or seven years old, the Prophet ﷺ said about them, "Al-Ḥasan and al-Ḥusayn are the masters of the youth of Paradise." He said this about them although they were still children. This means that although they were at that age, they had the understanding and knowledge of young men. Manners and honor cannot adequately describe them.

Had someone said, at that time, that this child would be killed by this Prophet's ﷺ umma without crime or fault, no one would have believed him. The Prophet ﷺ himself spoke this bitter truth and cried because of it, and everyone wondered about it at the time and were astonished that such a thing could happen.

Imām al-Ḥusayn عليه السلام in his Youth

The second period extended twenty-five years from the death of the Prophet ﷺ to the caliphate of the Commander of the Believers عليه السلام. During that time, Imām al-Ḥusayn عليه السلام was a robust, knowledgeable, and courageous young man who took part in wars and withstood hardships. Everyone knew how great he was, and whenever noble people were mentioned, his name came to mind among the Muslims of Mecca, Medina, and everywhere else Islam spread. All people respected and honored Imām al-Ḥusayn and his brother عليهما السلام, and even the caliphs of the time honored and revered them.

Imām al-Ḥusayn عليه السلام was an exemplar for the youth of his age. If someone had said that this young man would be killed by the umma, no one would have believed him.

The Estrangement of Ahl al-Bayt عليهم السلام

The third period is the period of Ahl al-Bayt's عليهم السلام estrangement following the martyrdom of Imām ʿAlī عليه السلام. At that time, Imām al-Ḥasan and Imām al-Ḥusayn عليهما السلام

lived in Medina. Twenty years after the killing of Imām ʿAlī ﷺ, the Imāmate of the Muslims fell to Imām al-Ḥusayn ﷺ even if he was actually deprived of the caliphate. This made people know him as a knowledgeable scholar, and their respect for him grew. He became a guiding post for anyone who wanted to hold fast to Ahl al-Bayt ﷺ.

He was a beloved, honorable, noble, knowledgeable man. He even sent a letter to Muʿāwiya. If anyone else had written that same letter, his fate would have been death. Nevertheless, when Muʿāwiya received Imām al-Ḥusayn's ﷺ letter, he read it with due respect and simply disregarded the parts that offended him. Had someone at the time said that Imām al-Ḥusayn ﷺ — this honorable, respected man who is the embodiment of Islam and the Qurʾān —would soon be killed a gruesome death by the umma of Islam and the Qurʾān, no one would have believed it. Nevertheless, this shocking and unimaginable thing did indeed happen.

But who did it? It was done by people who used to visit Imām al-Ḥusayn ﷺ and express their love and devotion to him. What does this mean? It means that over those fifty years, Islamic society was being voided of the truth of Islam and its values. It was an Islamic society externally, but internally it was hollow. At that time, prayers were being held, the Friday prayer was being observed, the umma was called the Muslim umma, and some of its members even supported Ahl al-Bayt ﷺ! This is where the danger lies.

The Love of Ahl al-Bayt ﷺ in the Islamic World

I assure you that the Islamic world as a whole believed and still believes in Ahl al-Bayt ﷺ. No one doubts this truth. The love of Ahl al-Bayt ﷺ is a common phenomenon among Muslims, past and present. Wherever you look in the Islamic world, you will find Muslims who love Ahl al-Bayt ﷺ. The Imām al-Ḥusayn Mosque and the Sayyidah Zaynab Mosque in Cairo are always crowded with visitors. Muslims go there, visit the tomb, kiss it, and seek intercession with God ﷻ through it. A year or two ago, a book about Ahl al-Bayt ﷺ was brought to me—there are many old books that discuss this topic but I mentioned this book because it is new—that was written by a contemporary scholar in Ḥijāz. This book proves that the Ahl al-Bayt ﷺ are Imām ʿAlī ﷺ, Sayyidah Fāṭimah ﷺ, Imām al-Ḥasan ﷺ, and Imām al-Ḥusayn ﷺ. This is a belief that inhabits our very souls as Shīʿas, but this Muslim brother who is not a Shīʿa wrote this book and published it. The book is still available and I have a copy of it myself. Thousands of copies must've been published and distributed. This means that Ahl al-Bayt ﷺ are respected and revered by all Muslims, and in their own era they were honored and loved to the utmost. Nevertheless, when a society becomes hollow, such an incident could indeed happen. What is the moral of the story? The moral is that we have to know what to do to keep society from slipping to such a level. This means that we have to understand the circumstances that led society to such an end. This is an extensive discussion whose summary I would like to relate to you.

The Pillars of the Prophetic Order

As a preface to my topic, I will point out that the Prophet ﷺ established a political order on various pillars. The most important of them are the following four:

1. Masterful unambiguous knowledge of religion, religious rulings, society, obligations, God ﷻ and His Prophet ﷺ, and nature.

This knowledge led to the accumulation of all sciences and led Islamic society to the height of urban life and scientific culture in the fourth Hijri century. The noble Prophet ﷺ made sure nothing was ambiguous or unclear. There are many marvelous Qurʾānic verses, but our time does not allow us to list them. Whenever anything ambiguous or unclear came up, a verse was revealed to explain it.

2. Absolute justice that is free of favoritism in judicial and public affairs, although when it came to his own rights, the Prophet ﷺ was clement. This means

that people were ruled with complete justice; the bounds (*ḥudūd*) of God ﷻ were also observed fairly, and positions and responsibilities were allotted fairly.

It goes without saying that justice does not mean equality. Don't confuse the two: equality may entail injustice sometimes, but justice means putting everything in its proper place and giving everyone their dues.

Justice at that time was perfect and unalloyed, and no person could be excluded from the bounds of justice.

3. Pure worship of God ﷻ that is free of any polytheism. This means worship in personal individual acts, worship in prayer whose purpose is to draw near to God ﷻ, worship in establishing society, the reigning order, the way of life, and social relations. This point itself requires extensive explanation.

4. Overwhelming love and fervent emotion. This is one of the main features of Islamic society; the love of God ﷻ and His love for people: "A people whom He loves and who love Him," "Indeed God loves the penitent and He loves those who keep clean," "If you love God, then follow me; God will love you." Love: love for one's wife and love for one's children. It is commendable (*mustaḥabb*) to kiss

> one's children and love them, to love one's wife, and to love one's Muslim brothers and endear oneself to them, but the greatest love of all is the love of the Prophet ﷺ and Ahl al-Bayt ؑ: “I do not ask you any reward for it except love of [my] relatives.”

Changing Pre-Islamic Society

The Prophet ﷺ set these outlines and established society upon them, preparing the features of government for ten years in this way. Of course, educating people can only happen gradually. Over those ten years, the Prophet ﷺ strove to strengthen society's pillars. Nevertheless, ten years is a very short time to teach people new habits, and the ways of pre-Islamic society were entirely opposed to these four pillars. This is because pre-Islamic society was devoid of knowledge, mired in the perplexity of ignorance and error, and was far from the worship of God ﷻ. It was a society of oppression and tyranny that was far from justice and full of injustice and discrimination.

In his second sermon in *Nahj al-Balāgha*, Imām ‘Alī ؑ drew a splendid picture of the injustice and discrimination of pre-Islamic society. He said, “They were trials (*fitan*) that stomped on the people with a nail and hoof.”

It was a loveless society; they buried their daughters alive, and every clan avenged its kinsmen by killing anyone of the killer's clan regardless of innocence or guilt. They were seized by oppression, cruelty, harshness, and rudeness.

The Prophetic Educational Model Continues

People who grew up in such a state may be reformed, educated, and introduced to Islam over ten years given the right circumstances, but its values and concepts do not become so rooted in them that they can inspire such a change in others.

People embraced Islam in large numbers, and some of them had not known the Prophet ﷺ. This highlights the importance of the testament (*waṣiyya*) in which the Shīʿas believe; the purpose of the testament and divine choice (*naṣṣ*) is to preserve this educational model. Clearly, it is not like regular testaments that we are familiar with. After all, every person leaves a last will and testament for his children before death. However, the testament we are concerned with is about the persistence of the Prophet's ﷺ path after his passing.

I don't want to get into theological arguments here. I only want to analyze history, and you should analyze it too. This discussion, of course, concerns everyone and is not limited to the Shīʿas. It concerns Sunnīs, Shīʿas, and all Muslim groups. Given its importance, they should all pay attention to it.

Let's consider the incidents that took place after the Prophet's ﷺ passing. What was the cause of society's regression in that way during fifty years? This is the heart of the matter, and we should look into what history says about it. Clearly, an edifice built by the Prophet ﷺ wouldn't collapse so easily. This is why everything continued as usual after his passing, except for the issue of the testament. Justice, contemplation, and worship were all well. If someone were to look at the general structure of Islam in those early years, he would find everything as it was, with no regression. It's true that some accidents happened every now and then, but on the whole, the same pillars and foundations set up by the Prophet ﷺ persisted. Things did not stay that way, however, and Islamic society gradually slipped toward weakness and emptiness.

The Path of Those Whom You Have Blessed

There is an issue concerning Sūrat al-Fātiḥa that I have pointed out many times on different occasions. When a person calls upon his Lord to "guide us on the straight path," he clarifies the meaning of the straight path by saying "the path of those whom You have blessed." God ﷻ has blessed many peoples and nations. He blessed the Children of Israel: "O Children of Israel, remember My blessing which I bestowed upon you." Divine blessing is not limited to prophets, the righteous, and the martyrs: "they are with those whom God has blessed, including the prophets and the truthful, the martyrs and the righteous." Those referred to in the verse also received divine blessing as well as the Children of Israel.

Those who receive God's ﷻ blessing are divided into two groups. When the first group is blessed, it does not incur God's ﷻ anger, act in a way to cause divine wrath, or stray from the straight path. This is the group we call upon God ﷻ to include us in. The phrase "such as have not incurred Your wrath" is actually a description of "those whom You have blessed." The adjective phrase modifying "those" is "such as have not incurred Your wrath."

As for the second group, they changed God's ﷻ blessing with ingratitude and refused it, incurring His wrath. They might have been people who followed the lead of ingrates and strayed from the straight path. Shīʿa narrations indicate that those who incurred God's ﷻ wrath were the Jews. This explanation is proven in reality. Up to the time of Prophet ʿĪsā عليه السلام, the Jews deliberately opposed Prophet Mūsā عليه السلام and his trustees (*awṣiyāʾ*, sing. *waṣī*). As for those who have gone astray, they are the Christians; they went astray when God ﷻ blessed them, or at least the majority of them did.

God ﷻ bestowed his blessing on the Muslims too, but this blessing became closer to divine wrath and error due to their own actions. This is why Imām Jaʿfar al-Ṣādiq عليه السلام has said, "God's wrath increased against the people of this earth when al-Ḥusayn was killed." This is because Imām al-Ḥusayn ﷺ is an infallible Imām. This means that a society that enjoys divine blessing could incur God's ﷻ wrath. For this reason, we must be extremely careful and cautious while we commit to the path; of course, this is a difficult thing that requires attention and vigilance.

After the Prophet ﷺ

In what follows, I will mention some examples. There is a difference between the elites and the masses. If the elites strayed, they would be included among those who incurred God's ﷻ wrath, whereas if the masses strayed, they would be included among the astray. History books are of course full of examples. Everything I will relate from now on comes from Ibn al-Athīr. I will avoid any Shīʿa sources and even any Sunnī authors who the Sunnīs cast doubts upon, such as Ibn Qutayba al-Dīnawarī, whose al-Imāma wal-siyāsa contains amazing things.

When you look at the contents of Ibn al-Athīr's *al-Kāmil fil-tārīkh*, you notice an Umayyad and an ʿUthmanī bias. I think the author chose to write in that style because of certain considerations. Speaking of the killing of ʿUthmān, this historian says that the people of Egypt, Kūfa, Baṣra, Medina, and others were the ones who killed ʿUthmān.

After relating various historical texts and reports, Ibn al-Athīr says, "For certain reasons, I have left out many things that people made excuses for killing ʿUthmān."

When he related the story of Abū Dharr and Muʿāwiya, and how Muʿāwiya made Abū Dharr travel from Shām to Medina without a saddle and then banished him from Medina to al-Rabadha in a horrible manner, he said, "Certain things took place that cannot be said." Based on this, Ibn al-Athīr either followed a method of self-censorship, as the modern expression goes, or he was a zealot. Either way, he was neither Shīʿa nor inclined to Shiʿism. In all probability, he was an Umayyad who supported ʿUthmān. I should repeat that everything I will relate from this point forward is from Ibn al-Athīr.

In what follows I will mention examples of the elites. How did the elites act over those fifty years so that things ended up the way they did? When I focus on the circumstances of the time, it appears to me that the four pillars of worship, knowledge, justice, and love had been shaken. I will give you some examples as they appeared in historical sources.

Ṭalḥa b. ʿAbdullāh

Saʿīd b. al-ʿĀṣ was an Umayyad and a relative of ʿUthmān. He became governor after al-Walīd b. ʿUqba b. Abī Muʿayṭ. You saw some scenes of al-Walīd's life in the TV series on Imām ʿAlī ﷺ. He was the one in whose presence the sorcerer was killed. Anyway, Saʿīd b. al-ʿĀṣ came to fix al-Walīd's mistakes.

One day, a man in Saʿīd's court said, "How generous Ṭalḥa is!" Ṭalḥa must have given someone money or performed some other act of generosity. Saʿīd said, "Anyone who owns an estate like al-Nashāstaj better be generous!" Al-Nashāstaj was a big estate near Kūfa that was owned by Ṭalḥa b. ʿAbdullāh, the Prophet's ﷺ companion, who was living in Medina at the time. Saʿīd then said, "By God, if I had what he has, you would've lived a good life!" Compare this situation to the time of the Prophet ﷺ and the early period after his death. Notice the life that the notables, governors, and companions were living and the way they viewed the world. Things became this bad in only ten or fifteen years.

Abū Mūsā al-Ashʿarī

The next example is the governor of Baṣra, Abū Mūsā al-Ashʿarī. He is famous for his role in the issue of arbitration (*taḥkīm*). He went up on the pulpit one day when he was governor as the people were preparing to go on a raid. He called the people and urged them to wage jihād and mentioned its merits. This made some people leave their mounts behind and decide to fight on foot in desire of further reward (thawāb). "They ran at their horses," meaning they shooed them away for depriving them of reward. The more reasonable people decided to wait and see how things went, saying, "We will not rush into anything. We will wait and see what he will do. If his deeds are like his words, we will do as he does." In this regard, Ibn al-Athīr said, "When he [Abū Mūsā al-Ashʿarī] went out, he took his possessions out of his palace in loads that needed forty mules to carry them." These loads comprised his valuables, which he had to take everywhere with him, even when he went to wage jihād. This is because there were no banks at that time, and government positions were meaningless; Abū Mūsā al-Ashʿarī could have received an order of removal from the caliph while waging jihād. If such a thing were to happen, he wouldn't have been able to return to Baṣra and take his belongings. This is why he had to carry his valuables on forty mules and take them to the battle with him.

Some people came to Abū Mūsā al-Ashʿarī, clung to his reins and said, "Carry us on some of these mounts and walk on foot as you were urging us to do." He hit them with his whip, and they let go of his reins. Of course, these people did not accept such treatment and went to ʿUthmān and complained to him, so ʿUthmān removed Abū Mūsā. Can it be believed that Abū Mūsā al-Ashʿarī, a companion of the Prophet ﷺ and an elite member of society, was like this?

Sa'd b. Abī al-Waqqāṣ

The third example is Sa'd b. Abī al-Waqqāṣ, the governor of Kūfa. It happened that Sa'd borrowed some money from the treasury (*bayt al-māl*) one day. This was because the treasury wasn't under the governor's control. During that time, the governor was chosen to govern and direct people's affairs while another person, directly accountable to the caliph, was responsible for financial affairs.

When Sa'd b. Abī al-Waqqāṣ became governor of Kūfa, the treasurer was 'Abdullāh b. Mas'ūd, who was a respected companion.

A while after Sa'd b. Abī al-Waqqāṣ borrowed money from the treasury with the permission of 'Abdullāh b. Mas'ūd, 'Abdullāh asked Sa'd to return it. Sa'd claimed he was insolvent and the two men exchanged harsh words and disputed. Hāshim b. 'Uqba b. Abī al-Waqqāṣ happened to be present; he was a companion of Imām 'Alī ﵇ and an honorable man. He said to them, "Both of you are companions of the Prophet ﷺ, and people are looking. Don't argue like this and try to settle the issue in some way." Ibn Mas'ūd, who was an honest man, asked for the assistance of some people to get the money out of Sa'd's house; this means that Sa'd actually had the money. When Sa'd knew about this, he also asked the assistance of some people to prevent this. A great dispute resulted from Sa'd b. Abī al-Waqqāṣ' stalling.

Saʿd b. Abī al-Waqqāṣ, who was one of the six participants in the shūrā, became like this in a few years. Ibn al-Athīr described the incident as follows, "This was the first dispute among the people of Kūfa." In other words, according to Ibn al-Athīr, the first dispute among the people Kūfa was caused by a man of the elites who was seized by such an ardent love for this world.

Marwān b. al-Ḥakam

The next example concerns the conquest of Africa. When the Muslims conquered Africa and divided the spoils among the men, they had to send the khums to Medina. It was a huge sum of money. Elsewhere, Ibn al-Athīr says that when this khums (from the spoils of war) arrived in Medina, Marwān b. al-Ḥakam bought it for 500,000 dinars. Although this was a fortune, the value of that khums was greater still. This became one of objections to ʿUthmān later on. Of course, ʿUthmān apologized and said that he only approved it because Marwān was one of his blood relations. ʿUthmān claimed he was honoring his blood relations (*ṣilat al-raḥim*) because Marwān was suffering hardship and needed help. The point here is that the elites sought to accumulate large amounts of money.

Al-Walīd b. ʿUqba

Another example is when ʿUthmān removed Saʿd b. Abī al-Waqqāṣ from his position as governor of Kūfa and appointed al-Walīd b. ʿUqba b. Abī Muʿayṭ, who was ʿUthmān's own relative. When al-Walīd arrived in Kūfa, the Kūfans wondered at his appointment because he was famous for his foolishness and corruption. The verse "If a profligate [person] should bring you some news, verify it" refers to al-Walīd. This means that the Qurʾān itself described al-Walīd as profligate because he brought forth news that harmed some people during the time of Prophet ﷺ.

Observe how standards and things changed. This person whom the Qurʾān that people read every day called profligate became governor. Both Saʿd b. Abī al-Waqqāṣ and ʿAbdullāh b. Masʿūd were surprised when they saw him coming to Kūfa as governor. When ʿAbdullāh b. Masʿūd saw him, he said, "Did you become righteous all of a sudden or did the people turn corrupt?" The cause of Saʿd b. Abī al-Waqqāṣ' wonder was different, for he asked him, "Did you become prudent all of a sudden or did we become foolish?" Al-Walīd replied to Saʿd, "Don't fret, Abū Isḥāq. It's neither. Monarchy is just fickle like that." Saʿd b. Abī al-Waqqāṣ, a companion of the Prophet ﷺ, was hurt by this remark and said, "I see. You've turned the caliphate into a monarchy."

Wilāya: The Government of Love

One day, 'Umar asked Salmān al-Fārisī, "Am I a king or a caliph?" Salmān was an esteemed and respected figure; he was one of the most senior companions, and his opinion was valued. He responded, "If you collected from the land of the Muslims a dirham or more or less and misused it, you would be a king and not a caliph."

Salmān showed 'Umar the standard that settles the matter. Ibn al-Athīr commented on this by saying, "'Umar cried." It was a really deep and meaningful lesson. The matter at stake here is the caliphate. Both the caliphate and the wilāya mean a government that is accompanied by love and connection to the people. They entail compassion and tenderness toward the people; their purpose is not to dominate or control. Monarchy, however, does not have such connotations; it has nothing to do with the people. A king is a domineering ruler who does whatever he wants.

This was the state of the elite, and this was where money drove them over the years. This happened even in the time of the rightly-guided caliphs (*al-khulafā' al-rāshidūn*) who put emphasis on holding fast to the rulings of Islam because they had lived a long time under the rule of the Prophet ﷺ whose echoes were still heard in Medina. It was a society in which a figure like Imām 'Alī b. Abī Ṭālib (a) was present, but when the center of the caliphate moved to Damascus, things went too far.

These are examples of the elites' lives at the time. If you dig into the Tārīkh of Ibn al-Athīr or other historical sources that our Sunnī brothers hold in high regard, you will find thousands and not just hundreds of other examples.

A Jew Speaks for Islam

When justice is lost and worship of God ﷻ disappears, it's natural for society to become hollow and for souls to become corrupt. Imagine a society where people chase after riches and the wreckage of this world so greedily. In that society, the person teaching people was Kaʿb al-Aḥbār, the Jew who later converted to Islam and did not live under the Prophet's ﷺ rule. He did not embrace Islam in the time of the Prophet ﷺ or in the time of Abū Bakr, but in the time of ʿUmar, and he died in the time of ʿUthmān! What kind of society is that?!

The word aḥbār is the plural of habr, meaning rabbi. This man was the head of the rabbis, and he made his way into Islam and took to speaking about Islamic issues. One day, he was sitting in the court of ʿUthmān, and Abū Dharr came in. He said something that angered Abū Dharr, so Abū Dharr said to him, "What are you doing here? Are you teaching us about Islam and its rulings although we heard them from the

Prophet ﷺ himself?" Standards were lost, criterias were confused, and values were undermined. Things were voided of their meanings and became superficial. Although they had raised the banner of Islam, worldliness and the love of money seized the people who lived a long time in might and abstinence of the world's frills. During such a time, culture and knowledge would become the task of a recent convert who portrayed Islam as anything that appealed to him regardless of the actual rulings of Islam. Some people even gave his opinion precedence over seasoned faithful people.

The Masses

That was the state of the elites. As for the masses, they always follow the elites and imitate them. For this reason, the worst mistake a well-known person could make is to deviate because his deviation would result in the deviation of many people. When these people see that the values are being distorted, the actions (of the elites) are in contradiction with their words and are in opposition of the sunnah of the Holy Prophet ﷺ, they will eventually follow the path of the elites, taking them as role models.

'Ammār b. Yāsir: A Man of Values

Let me give you an example. The governor of Baṣra wrote to the caliph telling him that the people of Baṣra were many and that the land tax (*kharāj*) was not enough to fill their needs, asking him to grant the people of Baṣra the land tax of two other cities. When the people of Kūfa heard about this, they asked their governor ʿAmmār b. Yāsir to do the same. ʿAmmār was an honorable man who remained as resolute as a mountain; of course, there were people who could not be shaken, but they were few. ʿAmmār refused, so the people of Kūfa detested him and complained to the caliph about him, which led to his removal. This also happened to Abū Dharr and others such as ʿAbdullāh b. Masʿūd. When such considerations are not kept in mind, a society becomes devoid of values. This is one of the morals.

Piety: Monitoring Oneself and Others

Know, dear ones, that a person only notices such social developments after a long time. This is why we must be careful about this and monitor the situation, which is the meaning of piety (*taqwa*). Piety is when those who have authority over their own selves are cautious for the sake of their own selves, and when those who have authority over their own selves and others are cautious for the sake of themselves and others. Those who are at a position of authority should be cautious for their own sakes and for the sake of society as a whole so that it wouldn't chase after the world and its frills. Such people should not be susceptible to the pitfall of selfishness (*ḥubb al-dhāt*). Of course, this doesn't mean that they need to neglect establishing society. To the contrary, they need to establish society and accumulate wealth, but not for their own sakes, because that is detestable. Anyone who is capable of increasing the wealth of society and achieving great things gains a great reward. In the past years, some people have been able to build up this country, undertake construction works, and achieve great things. This is a credit to them and not a manifestation of worldliness. Worldliness is when a person seeks his own advantage and welfare or thinks about collecting wealth for himself at the expense of others. This is detestable. We must be careful of such pitfalls. If we are not careful, society gradually slips toward losing its values and becomes an empty shell. In such a state, it could suddenly undergo a great trial like the revolt of Imām al-Ḥusayn عليه السلام and fail to measure up to it.

Rayy for al-Zahrāʾ عليها السلام's Beloved

ʿUmar b. Saʿd was offered the province of Rayy. At the time, Rayy was a vast and wealthy region. During the time of the Umayyads, the position of governor was not like the governors of today. Today governors are paid public servants who work hard, but things back then were different. Anyone appointed as governor had complete authority over his domain's riches after sending a portion of them to the capital. This is why the position of governor was extremely important.

The condition for making ʿUmar b. Saʿd governor was him fighting Imām al-Ḥusayn عليه السلام. Naturally, a noble person who has values wouldn't hesitate to refuse such an offer. What is the value of Rayy and other places? Even if the whole world were offered to a person, he should not so much as frown at Imām al-Ḥusayn عليه السلام, so what could be said about fighting al-Zahrāʾ عليها السلام's beloved عليه السلام and killing him and his children? This is what a person who has values would do. However, when society becomes hollow and devoid of values, and when principles become weak, the situation becomes dangerous. The most a person could do in such a situation is ask for some time to consider the offer. Even if a person would think for a whole year in such circumstances, he would reach the same conclusion and make the same decision. The time he would have asked for is pointless; at most, such a man would consider the matter for a night then declare his agreement. God عز وجل did not aid ʿUmar b. Saʿd to attain his goal, however, and the result of his action was the calamity of Karbalāʾ.

An Analysis of ʿĀshūrāʾ

I would like to say a word about the analysis of ʿĀshūrāʾ. A person like Imām al-Ḥusayn عليه السلام, who is an embodiment of all divine and humanitarian values, revolted to stand in the face of the widespread corruption in society that was threatening its very foundations. The degradation reached such a point that even if people wanted to live a dignified Islamic life, they wouldn't have had the means to do so. During such circumstances Imām al-Ḥusayn ﷺ stood steadfast with every fiber of his being against that increasing emptiness and corruption. He sacrificed himself, his loved ones, his children ʿAlī al-Aṣghar and ʿAlī al-Akbar, and his brother al-ʿAbbās for the sake of divine values. In the end, he achieved the desired result by reviving the way of his grandfather the Prophet ﷺ. This is the meaning of the Prophet's ﷺ saying, "... And I am from Ḥusayn." This is the other side of the story: Karbalāʾ is full of splendor. This eternal epic cannot be comprehended except through love. To understand the heroism and glory Imām al-Ḥusayn b. ʿAlī ﷺ achieved in one day and one night, from the afternoon of the ninth of Muḥarram until the afternoon of the tenth of it, you have to see with the lens of love. His heroism and glory have immortalized him forever; for this reason, all the efforts to erase the incident of al- Ṭaff have failed.

The Moral of ʿĀshūrāʾ[25]

How is ʿĀshūrāʾ a Moral Lesson?

Aside from being a lesson, ʿĀshūrāʾ is also a moral arena. We must contemplate it to understand these morals. What does this mean? It means comparing our own state and understanding our circumstances, the threats

---

[25] Sayyid Khāminaʾī's meeting with the ʿĀshūrāʾ regiments, brigades, and factions on 22/4/1371 SH.

we are facing, and the actions that are required of us. For example, if you were to see an overturned car, or two cars that got into an accident, and the passengers all died, you would stop and think about the moral of this accident. You would think about the car's speed and the reckless driving that resulted in such an ending. This is a different kind of lesson that comes from contemplation. Allow me to expand a little.

The First Moral

The first moral of ‘Āshūrā’ that interests us is that Imām al-Ḥusayn ؑ sacrificed himself to save Islamic society fifty years after the Prophet's ﷺ passing. Had his sacrifice come a thousand years after the formative years of Islam, in response to the nations that reject and oppose Islam, it would've been a different story. But Imām al-Ḥusayn b. ‘Alī ؑ was witnessing a situation in the heart of the Islamic world, i.e. Mecca and Medina, and the only solution he could see was offering the sacrifice of his own pure blood. What are the circumstances that made Imām al-Ḥusayn ؑ believe that Islam could not be revived and saved except through a sacrifice? Here lies the moral of the story.

The Prophet ﷺ was the leader of Islamic society. He sent Muslims carrying the banner of Islam from Mecca and Medina to the farthest ends of the Arabian Peninsula and Shām, threatening the Byzantine Empire and causing its armies to retreat. Meanwhile, the

Muslims returned to their own lands victorious. This happened in Tabūk, for instance. The verses of the Qur'ān came forth from the mosques and were heard in alleyways, and the Prophet ﷺ recited the verses of God ﷻ to the people, preached to them, and made every effort to lead them to the path of guidance.

What could have happened so that this society grew so distant from Islam and came to be ruled by Yazīd? In this situation, Imām al-Ḥusayn ؑ saw that his only option was to proceed with this grand sacrifice that is unprecedented in history. What happened for things to get this bad? Here lies the moral.

The Disease of Islamic Society

We must contemplate this deeply. Today we are also an Islamic society, so we must look into the disease that struck their society for it to be led by Yazīd. Kūfa was the seat of Imām 'Alī's ؑ rule, but twenty years after his martyrdom it witnessed the heads of his sons raised on spears and paraded in alleyways. What happened?

Kūfa was no stranger to religion; it was the city in whose markets Imām 'Alī ؑ walked, commanding the right and forbidding the wrong. From its mosques came the recitations of the Qur'ān night and day. This very same city later witnessed the daughters and womenfolk of Imām 'Alī ؑ held captive and paraded around the markets.

The Primary Factors of Deviation and Error

What happened in those twenty years for things to get this bad? What is this dangerous disease that could cause a society led by the Prophet ﷺ and Imām ʿAlī عليه السلام to reach such a fate in a few decades? We would do well to fear this disease.

Our great Imām قدس سره proudly considered himself a follower of the Prophet ﷺ. His pride comes from his ability to understand the rulings that the Prophet ﷺ brought, apply them, and spread them. However, the Prophet ﷺ is incomparable, even when Imām Khumaynī قدس سره is involved. The society that the Prophet ﷺ established suffered this disease after only a few years. Our own society must remain cautious not to suffer this disease itself. Here lies the moral.

We must diagnose the disease and consider it a grave danger to us in order to avoid it. I think this message of ʿĀshūrāʾ is the most important of its lessons and messages for us today. We have to diagnose the disease that struck that society so that the head of Imām al-Ḥusayn عليه السلام, the grandson of the Prophet ﷺ and the son of his caliph Imām ʿAlī عليه السلام, was paraded in the city once ruled by his father. No one even bothered to do anything about it. People headed from Kūfa itself toward Karbalāʾ to kill Imām al-Ḥusayn عليه السلام and his companions while they were thirsty and then took Imām ʿAlī's عليه السلام womenfolk captive!

Much can be said about this. A Qur'ānic verse comes to mind in answer to my question. The Qur'ān gave us the answer and determined the disease in the verse: "But they were succeeded by an evil posterity who neglected the prayer, and followed [their base] appetites. So they will soon encounter [the reward of] perversity."[26]

Neglecting the Mention of God ﷻ and Following Desires

The fundamental factors of this deviation and error are two. The first factor is neglecting the mention of God ﷻ, whose manifestation is prayer. This means forgetting God ﷻ, emptying life of its moral aspects, abandoning the direction toward God ﷻ, neglecting to contemplate and beseech Him, and erasing divine teachings from public life. The second factor is following base desires (*shahawāt*, sing. *shahwa*): "and followed [their base] desires" and the whims of the self. All of this may be summarized as loving this world, panting after riches and fortunes, and indulging in worldly pleasures.

The Loss of Principles

The loss of principles is a grave trial that could affect us too. If principles are gone or weakened within Islamic society, if we are consumed by infighting, and if we fear falling behind in worldliness, we would be giving our own interests precedence over the interests of society.

[26] Sūrat Maryam, Verse 59.

It's no wonder in such a case that things would get that bad!

The Islamic order is only crystalized, preserved, and driven forward by faith, unrelenting efforts, slogans, and rejuvenating and caring about Islamic rites. In contrast, weakening our own slogans, neglecting Islamic and revolutionary principles, and looking at matters materialistically would lead us to such a fate. The Muslims of the formative period of Islam faced such a trial.

When Standards are Reversed

There was a time for Muslims when the most important things were the progression of Islam, the pleasure of God ﷻ, the teaching of Islam and religious sciences, and knowing the Qurʾān. The ruling order and the administration of the state were characterized by abstinence, piety, disregarding the world and its frills, and giving up personal desires. The result was a magnificent movement toward God ﷻ. It is in such circumstances that a person like Imām ʿAlī b. Abī Ṭālib ؑ would be able to attain the caliphate and a person like Imām al-Ḥusayn b. ʿAlī ؑ would be revered. This would happen because both of them have the highest of standards.

When the standard is God ﷻ, piety, disregarding the world, and waging jihād in the way of God ﷻ, those who fulfill this standard present themselves and assume control of things. Only then does a society turn into an Islamic society. If the standards become reversed, however, and those who assume control are those who most love the world, follow desires, seek personal interests, and neglect honesty and trustworthiness, the result would be the rulership of people like ʿUmar b. Saʿd and ʿUbayd Allah b. Ziyād and the death of someone like Imām al-Ḥusayn b. ʿAlī ﵇.

Preserving the Standards

People who are careful should not allow the reversal of Islamic society's standards. If the standard of piety is shaken, the obvious result would be the shedding of pious blood like that of Imām al-Ḥusayn ﵇. If the benchmark becomes scheming, using force, and turning away from Islamic values, it is natural for a person like Yazīd to rule and for a person like ʿUbayd Allah b. Ziyād to become the number one man in Iraq.

Islam had to change these standards, and this is what our revolution has to do: changing false and incorrect standards that are ruling the world.

The world today is a world of tyranny, force, desires, and choosing the material dimension over the moral one. This is not even limited to the present. The moral aspects of society have been weakened for centuries now. Efforts have been made to destroy the moral dimension of things, so powerful people, materialists, and capitalists were brought to establish an order that controls religion. At the head of this order was America, the biggest liar and schemer that has nothing to do with human virtues. America is the cruelest toward other countries, followed by other powers, each according to its ability.

The Islamic Revolution and the Inspiration of 'Āshūrā'

One significance of the Islamic Revolution is reviving Islam and reviving the words: "Indeed the noblest (or 'the most honoured') of you in the sight of God is the most Godwary among you."[27] The Islamic Revolution came to demolish this erroneous edifice that is controlling the world and establish a new one. If the ruling order is materialistic, a corrupt, misguided, dour-faced person who chases his own desires like Mohammad Reza Pahlavi, is sure to rise to the highest levels of society. In such a world, a virtuous person like the Imām قدس سره is left to prison and exile. There would be no place left for the Imām قدس سره in society if it is ruled by force, corruption, fabrication, and vice; prison, detention, and death would be the fate of an honest, virtuous, spiritual man rooted in mysticism and connected to God ﷻ.

[27] Sūrat al-Ḥujurāt, Verse 13.

When things changed and a person like the Imām Khumaynī assumed responsibility, desires, worldliness, subordination, and corruption were replaced by piety, abstinence, purity, light, jihād, caring about humanity, chivalry, brotherhood, selflessness, and sacrifice. These virtues and values became the norm with the coming of the Imām.

Weakening and Isolating the Revolution

If we preserve these values, the system of the Imāmate will persist, and the likes of Imām al-Ḥusayn b. ʿAlī ﵇ will not be led to slaughter. However, a society might lose its values and mentality of mobilization and focus on personal luxuries instead of caring about obligations and divine principles. Such a society would isolate the sincere and faithful members of the mobilization, who only require the presence of an arena of jihād, and give authority to rude, greedy, insatiable, impure, and immoral people. In this case, everything would change. If the period between the passing of the Prophet ﷺ and the martyrdom of his grandson ﵇ was fifty years, this period might've been shorter had it happened in our time. These virtues would've been lost and its possessors would've been slaughtered. We must oppose the deviation that the enemy is imposing on us. In other words, the moral of ʿĀshūrāʾ is not to allow the isolation of the spirit of the Revolution and the sons of the Revolution in society.

What Caused the Incident of Karbalāʾ[28]

The Impurity that Polluted Society

I once spoke about the morals of ʿĀshūrāʾ. Back then, I said that in addition to the lessons ʿĀshūrāʾ teaches us, there are morals to be contemplated as well. Lessons teach us what to do, but morals show us how to deal with things that happened in the past and might happen in the future.

The moral of Imām al-Ḥusayn's ﷺ movement lies in contemplating history and observing what happened to that Islamic society that was led by the Prophet ﷺ. The Prophet ﷺ ruled for ten years with his extraordinary ability, aided by eternal divine inspiration and his own infinite wisdom. Then he was succeeded by Imām ʿAlī ﷺ who took Kūfa as the seat of this great rule. What happened? What is this impurity that struck the body of Islamic society and led to the killing of Imām al-Ḥusayn b. ʿAlī ﷺ so brutally half a century after the passing of the Prophet ﷺ and twenty years after the passing of Imām ʿAlī ﷺ?

How could something like this happen?

It wasn't something that happened to an unknown person. This was the very same boy the Prophet ﷺ

---

[28] Sayyid Khāminaʾī's lecture on 5/10/1374.

always hugged and kept by him at the pulpit while he spoke to the people. This is the grandson about whom the Prophet ﷺ said, "Ḥusayn is from me and I am from Ḥusayn." The relationship between grandfather and grandson was this close. This boy later became a pillar of Imām ʿAlī's ؑ government at the levels of war, peace, and politics; he was like the shining sun.

This influential figure, the Prophet's ﷺ grandson, with his piety, splendor, and school in Medina, was killed painfully while thirsty and besieged; this was how much society had deteriorated. This is despite the fact that he had admirers and followers all over the Islamic world. He wasn't killed alone; all the men who were with him and even his six-month old baby were killed. Afterward, his womenfolk and children were held captive like war-prisoners, paraded from town to town. So what happened? There is a moral here.

Compare our society and that society to find the differences. We are a society led by Imām Khumaynī ؒ who is without a doubt the greatest human being in our time. And yet our great Imām ؒ cannot even be compared to the Prophet ﷺ. The Prophet ﷺ had a great divine-given capacity to lead that society ten years after his death. Don't think that the conquests that took place were disconnected from the Prophet ﷺ; the ability of that great man was what led and is still leading Islamic society forward.

The Prophet ﷺ was present in that society's conquests and he is present in our society's victories.

I always tell the youths and the university and seminary students to take history seriously and contemplate it. This is because "that was a nation that has passed;" contemplating the past is a lesson that the Qur'ān teaches us. The heart of the matter lies in many different points that I cannot go into right now. I have already said enough about them, and the chance for research is available. Researchers only have to sit down and look into the details.

The Spread of Worldliness, Corruption, and Indecency

A primary cause is the spread of worldliness , corruption, and indecency, which stripped people of the feeling of religiosity, responsibility, and faith. The reason that I focus on corruption, indecency, jihād, and commanding the right and forbidding the wrong is that corruption and indecency make a society numb. Medina, which was the first seat of Islamic government, shortly became the destination of the best musicians, prostitutes, and dancers. Things got so far that if the court at Shām desired the most famous singers, it looked to Medina.

This audacity did not emerge after one hundred or two hundred years; it happened around the time Imām al-Ḥusayn (a) was martyred and even earlier. This was already happening during the time of Muʿāwiya! Medina became a center for corruption and indecency, polluting honorable and well-known families, including some Hashemite youths. Those in charge knew what they were doing. This was not limited to Medina; other regions were plagued by it too.

Beware the Storms of Corruption

This proves the necessity of holding fast to religion, piety, moral dimensions, God scrupulousness (*waraʿ*), and chastity (*ʿafāf*). This is why I have repeatedly urged our youth and advised them to beware the storms of corruption during our time.

Who is like the youths of Iran? In truth, these youths are the best of the best; they are at the forefront of knowledge, religion, and jihād. Where can we find their likes? The world does not contain many like them. We must beware of falling into corruption.

God ﷻ has preserved the sanctity of this revolution and its moral dimensions. Our youths are pure and chaste, but you should know that the frills and sweetness of this world are dangerous; they shake sturdy hearts and sturdy people. These whisperings (*wasāwis*, sing *wiswās*) have to be confronted, which is the greater jihād. You have fulfilled your lesser jihād to the utmost and now have to fulfill your greater jihād to the utmost.

Neglecting the Fate of Islam

The other factor that pushed circumstances this far is something that we witness even during the times of the Imāms' ﷺ followers. Even the followers of the Truth, the poles of wilāya and Shiʿism, had neglected the fate of the Islamic world and did not care about it. Some of them were eager to make a change, but the rulers were tyrannical. An example is the attack on Medina during the time of Yazīd, who sent an unjust man to suppress those who denounced him. This caused these objectors to give up their cause, retreat, and neglect everything. Of course, not all of them were from Medina, and disagreements spread among them.

The circumstances were entirely opposed to Islamic teachings: there was no unity, no organization, and no communication. The result of that was that the enemy fell upon them and killed them without mercy, and they retreated at the first confrontation. This is very important.

It's natural in the war between truth and falsehood for truth and falsehood to exchange blows. Just as truth attacks falsehood, falsehood attacks truth, and this keeps going until one side is exhausted and defeated.

The Secret to the Continuation of the Prophets' Knowledge

The secret behind the persistence of all the prophets' knowledge until today is monotheism, virtues, and religious values. These branches of knowledge are widespread among us today; wherever you look, you will see the knowledge of the prophets. It should be mentioned that all but a few prophets were oppressed. Consider how Prophet Mūsā ﷺ was oppressed or how Prophet 'Īsā ﷺ was chased and pressured, and yet their knowledge remained until our own day.

The secret is that the prophets did not abandon their duties, and the failure of one did not tempt another to surrender to falsehood. All the prophets , except a few, have suffered the blows of their enemies. They were killed, burned, imprisoned, or sawed alive, withstanding bitter torture at the hands of tyrants, and yet here is the world, under the banner of the prophets. Wherever you look, you will notice the knowledge of the prophets. Good morals and lofty terms like justice and peace are the fruit of the knowledge of the prophets. The secret is not getting tired and abandoning the field.

This steadfastness was absent during the time of Imām al-Ḥusayn ﷺ, which resulted in a disastrous calamity. Due to the lack of steadfastness, there was also a lack of communication. They quickly felt defeated and tired, and they left the field. The result was that the enemy was able to move forward.

Imām Khumaynī's ؒ Inspiration from Karbalā'

Inspiration was drawn from the experience of Karbalā' only once but it resulted in a resounding victory. This was during our Islamic Revolution. God ﷻ created our great Imām ؒ in such a way that he never felt defeat or fatigue, and failure never found its way into his heart. He believed in moving forward even in the darkest times. You experienced this personally during the eight years of the war when he didn't retreat even during the toughest times. He was as unwavering as a mountain. If a person was supported by an unwavering mountain, he would be reassured while fighting. Imām Khumaynī ؒ was like this throughout the struggle against the Pahlavi regime. He continued his jihād despite failures, difficulties, blows, pressures, exile, and old age. When the Imām ؒ began his jihād he was not a young man; he was sixty-three. I remember a speech of his in 1341 SH (1962 AD) when he said, "Why should I be afraid and who should I be afraid of? If they kill me at sixty-three —and this was the age of the Prophet ﷺ and Imām 'Alī ؑ when they departed from this world—I will be gone from this world. Is there happiness greater than this?" This was how he thought.

A Sturdy Mountain

The Imām ☪ was sixty-three when his jihād began. When the circumstances were right, he was ready to withstand hardships even in old age. He led the revolution, in all of its great incidents, from his eighties to his nineties. You witnessed this. He was not shaken by the threats of the U.S. and the USSR and their alliance, nor by the eight years of war and the economic, journalistic, and political siege. "Storms do not move him." No storm could shake Imām Khumaynī ☪, and he was victorious.

This experience was applied only once during our Revolution when our struggling people stood resolutely behind that great man. Even weak people joined this procession until the enemy was defeated, and our enemy is being defeated yet again today.

Where Do You Stand?[29]

Considering the Concerns

The Qur'ān invites us to contemplate the past and the morals of history. Some pedants, however, might say that history cannot be an example for the present. Such people aim to present their opinions as philosophical

---

[29] Sayyid Khāmina'ī's meeting with the officers and members of the 27th Muḥammad Rasūlullāh Brigade

propositions, but they fail at it. Let's not bother with such people.

The Qurʾān is truthful and reliable, and it calls upon us to draw morals from history. Drawing morals from history entails this state of concern that I alluded to before. If we were to contemplate the morals of history, we would have some concerns. These concerns relate to the future: what are they and what happened throughout history?

The Morals of ʿĀshūrāʾ

The incident of ʿĀshūrāʾ happened in the formative period of Islam. I mentioned before that the umma should contemplate the reason that society reached such a state only fifty years after the death of the Prophet ﷺ. The members of this umma, its viziers, commanders, leaders, scholars, judges, and Qurʾān reciters gathered in Kūfa and Karbalāʾ and tore the Prophet's ﷺ beloved apart in that horrible manner.

We must deeply contemplate the reasons that led to this state. I already spoke about this two or three years ago in a talk entitled, "The Morals of ʿĀshūrāʾ." Of course, this is different from the lessons of ʿĀshūrāʾ, such as courage, selflessness, and so on. The morals of ʿĀshūrāʾ are more important than the lessons of ʿĀshūrāʾ.

I already mentioned that things got to an extent that the womenfolk of the Prophet ﷺ were paraded around in streets and markets for all to see while being called rebels (*khawārij*). The term khawārij in Islam is given to those who rebel against the just Imām and disobey him, and who deserve the curse of God ﷻ, His Prophet ﷺ, and the faithful. These are the khawārij. This is why Muslims detested all khawārij: "It is lawful to shed the blood of anyone who rebels against a just Imām." This is although Islam places great sanctity on life.

They spread the idea that the Prophet's ﷺ grandson and the son of Imām ʿAlī and Sayyidah Fāṭimah عليهما السلام had rebelled against the just Imām. That just Imām was none other than Yazīd b. Muʿāwiya, and the people believed them!

The ruling class was composed of unjust people who said whatever they liked, but why did people believe them and stay silent about them?

Why Did the Islamic Umma Suffer Obliviousness and Humiliation?

What causes me concern is this: why did things get so bad? Why did the Islamic umma that was knowledgeable about Islamic rulings and the verses of the Qurʾān become oblivious and lax, which led to such a calamity? This is a cause for concern. Are we stronger and more determined than the society of the Prophet ﷺ

and Imām ʿAlī ؑ? What can we do to avoid repeating history?

No one answered my question about the causes, but I have the answer myself. I must say that no one has spoken about this topic before, or if anyone did, it wasn't discussed enough.

Today I would like to briefly discuss this. I will speak briefly about the root causes, offering you headlines that you should think about and that intellectuals and researchers should look into. We should come up with ways to prevent the recurrence of ʿĀshūrāʾ.

History Must Not Repeat Itself

If you and I do not stand up to these causes today, don't be surprised if our Islamic society reaches that state fifty or five or ten years later. We need sharp eyes that see beyond exteriors, honest hands that point the way, intellects that direct matters, and iron wills that stand by this path. This establishes a sturdy shield that cannot be penetrated. If we show neglect, the same thing will happen again, and all the blood that was spilled will be wasted.

During that time, things got so bad that the son and grandson of those killed by Imām ʿAlī ؑ, Ḥamza, and the other leaders of Islam, was in the Prophet's ﷺ place.

He put the head of the Prophet's ﷺ beloved before him, striking his incisors with a stick and reciting:

"I wish my ancestors of Badr had witnessed the panic of the Khazraj as the spears fell."[30]

The Qurʾān commands us to reflect as mentioned in the verse: "Say, 'Travel over the land."[31] It is telling us, "Observe what happened and beware." I am speaking to you briefly about this topic today so that intellectuals, researchers, and important people could make it a mainstream part of our country's culture if God ﷻ wills it.

The Masses and the Elites in Society

Notice, dear ones. If you look at any human society, in any city or country, people will be divided, according to a certain point of view, into two categories.

The first category acts based on thought, understanding, consciousness, and determination, knowing its path and committing to it. It does not concern us here whether this path is right or wrong. This category is the category of the elites.

---

30 Translator's note: This was first recited by ʿAbdullāh b. al-Zibiʿrā when he was still a polytheist as he gloated after the Battle of Uḥud.

31 Sūrat al-ʿAnkabūt, Verse 20.

The other category does not pause to determine the right path and stance. It does not care about analyzing, understanding, calculating, and knowing things. It simply follows the status quo and the whims of the time. This is the category of the masses. This means that society may be divided into masses and elites. This should be well-known.

Who are the elites? Are they a separate class? No, because this category that we call the elites may contain educated and uneducated people. The elites may include an uneducated person who nevertheless understands what he has to do. He works according to a plan and determination. Even if he did not go to school, get a degree, or dress like scholars, he understands the truth of things.

When the Revolution was still underway, before its victory, I was in exile in Iranshahr. In a nearby city, there was a group of people among whom was a driver. They were cultured and knowledgeable people. Although they were considered among the masses, they were actually of the elites. They used to come and visit me regularly in Iranshahr, telling me about the talks they had with a religious scholar in their city, who was a good man but was one of the masses!

Did you see? A truck driver was a member of the elites whereas that esteemed scholar and prayer leader was one of the masses. That scholar used to ask, “When the

Prophet ﷺ is mentioned, you say ṣalawāt only once, but when Imām Khumaynī ﵀ is mentioned, you say ṣalawāt three times. Why do you do that? Where's your understanding?" The truck driver responded, "When we are done with our fight and Islam dominates the whole world, and when the Revolution is victorious, we will no longer say ṣalawāt three times or even one time after Imām Khumaynī ﵀ is mentioned. These three ṣalawāt are a way of standing up to our enemies." Although the man was only a driver, he knew the truth of things while the scholar was oblivious.

The Characteristics of the Elites

I mentioned this example to let you know that when we say "elites" this does not mean a special class with a particular dress code. The elites could be men, women, rich, poor, government workers, or opposers of a tyrannical government. The elites may be righteous or wicked, and we will further divide them into subgroups.

When the elites do something, they take a stand. They choose their way after thought and analysis, which means that they understand and make decisions. These are the elites. Those on the other side are the masses.

The masses go with the status quo and don't analyze matters. If they see people chanting, "long live so and so" they chant with them, and when people chant "death to so and so" they chant with them. They walk any way without thought!

The Masses go as Things go

Muslim b. ʿAqīl came to Kūfa. The people said, "Here comes Imām al-Ḥusayn's cousin; here comes the Hashemites' messenger. He's intent on uprising and revolt!" They got excited, rallied around him, and pledged allegiance to him. Eighteen thousand men pledged allegiance to him. Five or six hours later, the heads of the tribes came to Kūfa and told the people, "Why did you do this? Who are you defending and against whom? You will pay dearly!" First, each of the tribal leaders went home. Then, the men of Ibn Ziyād surrounded Ṭawʿa's house to capture Muslim, and all those excited men turned against him.

This is the behavior of the masses; it's not the result of thought or sound analysis. They follow the status quo.

The Elites: Between Truth and Falsehood

In other words, in every society there are elites and masses. Let's leave the masses aside and look at the elites.

The elites are divided into two groups: the elites of the truth and the elites of falsehood. Isn't that so? Some people of culture, thought, and knowledge work for the truth because they have known the truth and its side so they work for that side. This means that they know the truth and are able to determine it. This is one group. The other group stands opposite to the truth.

If we go back to the formative period of Islam, there was the group of Imām 'Alī ﷺ, Imām al-Ḥusayn ﷺ, and the Hashemites on one hand, and the group of Mu'āwiya on the other. Both groups contained elites. There were intelligent and wise people on the side of the Umayyads; they were of the elites.

This means that the elites in any society are of two kinds: elites that support the truth and elites that support falsehood. What could be expected from the elites that support falsehood? Only conspiracy against the truth and the people. This is what should obligate you to fight the elites who support falsehood. This is a matter that is non-negotiable.

The Elites and the Truth

Now we come to discuss the elites who support the truth. I'm talking to you today; look at yourselves to see where you stand. When we say that the main thing is forethought and following a path based on vision, we are not confusing history and stories. History is the other side of our life.

History means you and I; it means those present here today. If we are the ones presenting and explaining history, each of us consider his position in this story. After that, we should see what those who were in a similar position did so that we don't make the same mistakes. In military science, there is an opposing side and our own side. If we look at our side's past plans, we might find that those who made the plans made certain mistakes. When we want to plan, we must not repeat them. If the plan itself was sound but someone on the battlefield did something wrong, we must not repeat his mistake. This is how history works. Now look into yourselves and find the formative period of Islam within.

Some people of the masses cannot make a decision, and their affairs are left to chance. If they happen to live in a time when they are led by someone like Imām 'Alī ؑ or Imām Khumaynī ؒ and are guided to Paradise, well and good. If righteous people lead them, they will end up in Paradise if God ﷻ wills it.

The Qur'ān tells us, "We made them leaders who invite to the Fire," "Have you not regarded those who have changed God's blessing with ingratitude, and landed their people in the house of ruin?" If similar people were present during such a time as 'Āshūrā', they would lead the masses to the Fire.

Beware of Being Part of the Masses

For this reason, beware of being part of the masses. This doesn't mean that you have to undertake advanced studies. Not at all. Many completed their higher studies but are counted among the masses. Many studied the religious sciences and are of the masses. Rich and poor people both belong to the masses. Whether we belong to the masses or not depends on us. We must be careful. Every deed that we do must be out of insight. If you act without insight, you belong to the masses. This is why the Qurʾān portrays the Prophet ﷺ as saying, "I summon to God with insight—I and he who follows me."

So reflect: are you of the masses or not? If you find that you are, hasten to leave their ranks. Try to cultivate the capacity of analysis, understanding, and knowledge.

If we are of the masses, do we support the truth or falsehood? The answer is clear: the elites of our society are certainly supporters of the truth, as they call to the Qurʾān, the Prophetic sunna, Ahl al-Bayt عليهم السلام, God ﷻ, and Islamic values. This is the Islamic Republic. This means that we are not talking about the elites who support falsehood; they do not concern us for the moment. The talk centers around the elites who support the truth, and this is where the trouble starts.

Difficult Trials

Know, dear ones, that the elites who support the truth are divided into two groups. The first group emerges victorious in the struggle against the temptations of life such as glory, desire , riches, pleasure, luxury, and reputation while the second group loses. All of these things are good in themselves, and are of life's delights: "the enjoyment of the life of this world." When the Qur'ān describes them as the enjoyment of this world, this means that they are not detestable. God ﷻ gave us enjoyment for our delight. If a person excessively indulges in these enjoyments to an extent that he cannot go without them, even if his financial situation demands it, that's one thing, but if he can go without them during any difficult test, that's another thing. These are matters that require consideration and precision. The future of society, order, and the Revolution can't be guaranteed randomly. Every society has these two groups of elites who support the truth. If the people who can forgo the enjoyments of this world, when required, are more numerous, what occured in the time of Imām al-Ḥusayn ؑ will not occur again, and you may be sure that our future is guaranteed forever.

The Elites and Attachment to this World

Sometimes the elites who support the truth are more numerous, but they become weak before worldly temptations, including riches, houses, fame, positions, and glory. They abandon the path of God ﷻ for selfish reasons and keep quiet when the truth needs to be told to save themselves, their positions, jobs, riches, children, families, relatives, and friends. If these types of elites are more numerous, we are in big trouble. If that were to happen, then those who walk in the footsteps of Imām al-Ḥusayn ؑ will be martyred and led to slaughter, and the followers of Yazīd will come to power. The Umayyads will rule the government that was established by the Holy Prophet ﷺ for a thousand years, and the Imāmate will turn into a monarchy.

Islamic Society Turns into a Monarchy

Islamic society is a society based on the Imāmate. This means that an Imām will be at the head of authority. People follow this Imām out of heartfelt love that stems from faith. A worldly ruler, however, rules people using oppression and force, and the people don't believe in him, accept him, or like him. When I say "the people" here, I mean the people of understanding and awareness.

The Umayyads turned the Imāmate in Islam into a ruling monarchy, and they ruled this expansive Islamic state for a thousand months, or ninety years.

Their edifice had a shaky foundation, ending in the revolt against them and their erasure from existence.

They were replaced by the Abbasids who ruled the Islamic world for six centuries, pretending to be the Prophet's ﷺ successors!

The Abbasid caliphs, or more accurately the Abbasid kings, indulged in corruption, profligacy, pleasures, wine, immorality, indecency, abominations (*khabā'ith*), and riches. Amusements, pleasures, and other forms of corruption were even present inside mosques. This is the way of all kings in the world. Despite this, the Abbasids led the people in prayer, and the people prayed behind them out of compulsion. Perhaps they weren't even compelled. Perhaps they were misinformed, which led to distorting their beliefs.

Curse the Planters of the First Seed

If most or all of the elites who support the truth in any society worry about losing their lives, riches, positions, glory, and social status, and fear isolation due to their attachment to this world, they will not be supporters of the truth who are ready to sacrifice themselves. When things get this bad, the natural consequence is the tragic martyrdom of Imām al-Ḥusayn ؑ, and the conclusion would be the domination of the Umayyads, Marwanīs, Abbasids, and the rest of the rulers that controlled the Islamic world until this day.

Look at the Islamic world and at some Islamic countries, and notice how their rulers are profligate and immoral. The rest of the world is like this too. This is why in the visitation of 'Āshūrā' you say, "O God, curse the first tyrant who usurped the rights of Muḥammad and the family of Muḥammad." That's the truth.

We have now managed to analyze the incident of 'Āshūrā' and its many morals. After this introduction, let's move on to history.

Material Privileges Cause the Elite to Slip

The slipping of the elites who supported the truth began six or seven years after the passing of the Prophet ﷺ. My talk here is regardless of the issue of the caliphate. The caliphate is a separate issue. I will now speak about this issue because it's dangerous. All these troubles happened seven years after the death of the Prophet ﷺ. The first signs of trouble appeared when they said that those who had precedence (*sābiqa*) in Islam, i.e. the Prophet's ﷺ companions who fought alongside him, should not be equated with the rest of the people; they should have privileges! And so they were given financial privileges out of the treasury!

This was the first misstep. All deviant trends begin with a small thing then worsen and grow. The deviations began at that point and continued until the time of 'Uthmān. During the reign of the third caliph, major companions became the richest of the rich. I mean well-known companions such as Ṭalḥa, al-Zubayr, Sa'd b.

Abī al-Waqqāṣ and other celebrated companions who became Grade A capitalists! When one of them died and his money was distributed over his heirs, they had to use axes to break the bars of gold, which he made out of melted gold, in the same way firewood is broken. How much gold did they have for them to need axes to break it apart?! And this gold was weighed using big scales; this is what history tells us!

The Causes of the Problems During Imām 'Alī's ﷺ Rule

This is not something that the Shī'as alone mention in their books. Everybody recorded this. The sums that they left behind were astronomical. This is what led to some incidents during Imām 'Alī's ﷺ rule. Because some people began to give great importance to status, they clashed with him.

By that point, twenty-five years had passed since the Prophet's ﷺ death, and many mistakes and dubious things were beginning to surface. As we know, Imām 'Alī ﷺ and the Prophet's ﷺ are the same. Without this twenty-five-year period, Imām 'Alī ﷺ wouldn't have had any trouble in establishing his intended society. However, he was facing a society in which some people were "taking turns in appropriating the money of God, taking His servants as slaves, and creating innovations in His religion." It was a society where values were lost to worldliness, and Imām 'Alī ﷺ was facing great difficulties in urging people to wage jihād.

The Elites Caused Imām al-Ḥusayn and Imām ʿAlī ﷺ Great Pain

Most of the elites supported the truth during the time of Imām ʿAlī ﷺ in that they knew it. However, they preferred this world over the Hereafter. This pushed Imām ʿAlī ﷺ into three battles, and he spent his rule of four years and nine months in these battles until he was martyred at the hands of a wretched man.

Imām ʿAlī's ﷺ blood is as precious as Imām al-Ḥusayn's ﷺ. In the visitation of ʿĀshūrāʾ, you read, "Peace upon you, O vengeance of God and son of His vengeance." This means that God ﷻ is the guardian of the blood (*walī al-damm*) of Imām al-Ḥusayn ﷺ and his father. This is a merit not given to anyone except the two of them.

It's well-known that there is a guardian for any blood that is spilled; this person is called walī al-damm. A father is the guardian of his son's blood, and a son is the guardian of his father's blood. This is vengeance for the Arabs.

Claiming the blood and its rights is vengeance for the Arabs. The one who will claim the blood of Imām al-Ḥusayn ﷺ and Imām ʿAlī ﷺ is God ﷻ. God ﷻ is the guardian of their blood.

These circumstances led to the martyrdom of Imām ʿAlī. After him came his son Imām al-Ḥasan who could only withstand the situation for six months because his companions abandoned him and left him to his fate. He saw that if he went through with fighting Muʿāwiya with such a small handful of people and he was martyred, no one would even seek to avenge him. This was because of the pervasiveness of moral degradation in Islamic society, even among the elites! Imām al-Ḥasan knew that Muʿāwiya's propaganda, money, and tricks will lure everyone, and that a year or two later people would say that Imām al-Ḥasan acted poorly when he stood up to Muʿāwiya. This meant that Imām al-Ḥasan's blood would have gone to waste. For this reason, Imām al-Ḥasan withstood all hardships and did not go into the arena of martyrdom.

The Most Difficult Choice

You know that martyrdom is sometimes easier than staying alive. People of wisdom and precision who possess moral horizons know this. Sometimes life and work in certain circumstances are a lot harder than death, martyrdom, and meeting God. Imām al-Ḥasan walked this difficult path. At that time, the elites were in a state of ruin and were not willing to join any movement. When Yazīd came into power, Imām al-Ḥusayn revolted against him; this is because Yazīd's bad traits made it easy to fight him. The blood of anyone who fought Yazīd would not go to waste.

During Yazīd's reign the only choice was the choice of revolt. In the time of Imām al-Ḥasan عليه السلام, in contrast, there were two choices: martyrdom or life. During that time, staying alive had a greater reward and purpose and was more difficult. Imām al-Ḥasan عليه السلام chose this more difficult path, but the time of Imām al-Ḥusayn عليه السلام was different. Imām al-Ḥusayn عليه السلام had only one choice, and staying alive amounted to not revolting, which was unreasonable. He had to revolt regardless of whether he came into power or became a martyr. He had to outline the path and highlight its significance so that it would be clear in case things deteriorated again.

The Elites' Crucial Role

Well, when Imām al-Ḥusayn عليه السلام revolted not many elites came to his aid despite his great status in Islamic society. Notice how big is the damage that's caused by the elites in society. They preferred this world over the fate of the Islamic world for centuries to come despite Imām al-Ḥusayn's عليه السلام status and popularity.

I was looking into the circumstances of Imām al-Ḥusayn's عليه السلام revolt and departure from Medina, and I noticed that ʿAbdullāh b. al-Zubayr also departed from Medina. Both were in the same situation, but ʿAbdullāh b. al-Zubayr cannot be compared to Imām al-Ḥusayn عليه السلام! Imām al-Ḥusayn's عليه السلام words alone made al-Walīd, the governor of Medina, speak gently to him and not resort to harshness. Whenever Marwān spoke, Imām al-

Ḥusayn ﵇ responded to him angrily and threatened him. Marwān, humiliated, could do nothing but keep quiet.

These two men themselves went and surrounded ʿAbdullāh b. al-Zubayr's house. ʿAbdullāh sent out his brother to ask their permission to walk alongside them. However, they insulted Ibn al-Zubayr and threatened him with death if he didn't come out. In the end, ʿAbdullāh b. al-Zubayr gave in to them and begged them to allow him to send his brother with them and come himself the next day.

The Greatness of Imām al-Ḥusayn ﵇

Although ʿAbdullāh b. al-Zubayr was also a prominent figure, his stance couldn't be more different from Imām al-Ḥusayn's ﵇. No one would have dared to treat Imām al-Ḥusayn ﵇ this way given his sanctity, greatness, majesty, and spiritual influence.

On his way to Mecca, anyone who saw Imām al-Ḥusayn ﵇ along the way used to address him with expressions such as "may I be made ransom for you," and "may my father and mother be ransom for you." That was how they spoke to Imām al-Ḥusayn ﵇; he had a special status in Islamic society. ʿAbdullāh b. Muṭīʿ came to him and said, "O son of the Prophet of God ﷺ, if you are killed, we will be as good as lost." He meant to say that the only thing stopping these people from harming us is their fear and awe of you; if you revolted and were killed, they would take us as their slaves.

Imām al-Ḥusayn ﷺ had a commanding authority that ʿAbdullāh b. ʿAbbās, ʿAbdullāh b. Jaʿfar, and even ʿAbdullāh b. al-Zubayr submitted to. Although ʿAbdullāh b. al-Zubayr worried about Imām al-Ḥusayn's ﷺ motives, he revered and honored him.

All the great personalities and elites who supported the truth, who weren't on the side of the Umayyads, and did not mix with the people of falsehood were discouraged when they sensed the ruling authority's tyranny. They backed down to preserve their lives, money, and positions. Many of them were even Shīʿas who believed in the Imāmate of Imām ʿAlī ﷺ and considered him the first rightful caliph. As a result of these people's discouragement, the masses leaned toward the side of falsehood.

The Masses Follow the Elites

If we look at the name of the Kūfans who wrote to Imām al-Ḥusayn ﷺ and asked him to come to Kūfa, they were all elites, known personages, and notables. The number of letters was huge, spanning hundreds of pages and perhaps filling several saddle bags. The people who wrote these letters were often notables, and their language shows how many truth-supporting elites were prepared to sacrifice their religion for this world. We can sense this from the letters.

Since those who preferred to sacrifice their religion for this world were more numerous, the result was Muslim b. ʿAqīl's death in Kūfa after he had received pledges of allegiance from eighteen thousand men, and ultimately the death of Imām al-Ḥusayn ﷺ in Karbalāʾ.

The Importance of the Elites

This means that the movement of the elites influences the movement of the masses. I don't know if this great truth is apparent enough for us; conscious people should always keep it in mind. You must have heard about what happened in Kūfa. Its people wrote letters telling Imām al-Ḥusayn ﷺ, "Come to us and we will treat you with due honor." The Imām ﷺ sent Muslim b. ʿAqīl to them to know the truth of the situation. If it was favorable, Imām al-Ḥusayn ﷺ was going to go to them himself.

Muslim came to Kūfa, entered the homes of Shīʿa notables, and read Imām al-Ḥusayn's ﷺ letter to them. People came in groups to Muslim and pledged their allegiance to him. The governor of Kūfa at the time, al-Nuʿmān b. Bashīr, was a mild and weak man; he announced that he would not go after anyone unless he was targeted personally and left Muslim in peace. The people saw that it was safe so they came to Muslim and pledged their allegiance to him.

Some of the elites who supported falsehood, along with the Umayyads, sent a letter to Yazīd letting him know that if he cared about Kūfa, he had better appoint a stern man as governor. They told him that al-Nu'mān b. Bashīr was powerless against Muslim b. 'Aqīl. Because of this, Yazīd wrote to 'Ubayd Allah b. Ziyād, who was governor of Baṣra, and told him that he was now governor of Kūfa while keeping his post over Baṣra as well. 'Ubayd Allah b. Ziyād immediately departed from Baṣra to Kūfa. The role of the elites is further clarified through examples of his arrival to Kūfa. If our time allows, we might discuss this further.

The Masses Move Without Thinking

'Ubayd Allah reached the outskirts of Kūfa at night. As soon as the people saw a man covering his face, coming with horses and arms, the masses among them thought he was Imām al-Ḥusayn ﷺ. They simply walked up to him and saluted him saying, "Peace be upon you, son of the Prophet of God ﷺ." These are the masses: they lack the capacity to analyze and consider. As soon as they saw a man coming with horses and arms, they thought he was Imām al-Ḥusayn ﷺ before he even said one word to them. Everyone started saying that he was Imām al-Ḥusayn ﷺ, but they should've paused to make sure of his identity.

This newcomer paid no attention to the people and went on to the governor's palace. When he got there, he entered the palace and introduced himself then began planning to quash Muslim b. ʿAqīl's mission. He focused his efforts on using the harshest pressures, threats, and torture against Muslim's supporters. Ibn Ziyād tricked Hāniʾ b. ʿUrwa into coming to the palace and then hit his head and face. When people crowded around the castle, ʿUbayd Allah b. Ziyād used trickery and lies to disperse them. This proves the role of corrupt elites who are supporters of the truth in name only. It's true that they know the truth, but they prefer this world over their religion.

Ibn al-Athīr mentions that the supporters of Muslim b. ʿAqīl were thirty thousand, and that there were four thousand of them with their swords at the ready around the house he was in. This was on the ninth of Dhū al-Ḥijja. When Muslim set out with a large number of his supporters, ʿUbayd Allah b. Ziyād sent some elites of falsehood to instill fear in them and spread the word that the Umayyads had everything at their command—arms, money, and power—while they themselves had nothing. Panic took hold of the people and they began to abandon Muslim b. ʿAqīl. By the time of the evening prayer, Muslim was left all alone, and ʿUbayd Allah b. Ziyād's crier told the people that everyone was to report to the mosque of Kūfa and pray. The historical sources say that the mosque was crowded with people who came to pray behind Ibn Ziyād.

The Inaction of the Elites on the Side of the Truth

Well, why did matters get that bad? When I look at it, I believe that the cause was that some elites of the truth chose a path of discouragement. One example of this is al-Qāḍī Shurayḥ. This Shurayḥ was not an Umayyad, and he understood how things were and knew on whose side the truth was. When they took Hāniʾ b. ʿUrwa and wounded his face and head then threw him in prison, Hāniʾ's clan quickly surrounded Ibn Ziyād's palace. Ibn Ziyād feared the consequences of this as they would say that he killed Hāniʾ himself. For this reason, he ordered Shurayḥ to go to the prison and see that Hāniʾ was alive with his own eyes.

Shurayḥ went and saw that Hāniʾ was alive but wounded. As soon as Hāniʾ saw Shurayḥ, he asked the aid of the Muslims and said to him, "Where are my people? Are they killed? Why haven't they come and saved me?"

Shurayḥ said that he wanted to go and give those surrounding the governor's palace Hāniʾ's message, but unfortunately ʿUbayd Allah b. Ziyād's spy was there too, so he couldn't. What does this "he couldn't" mean? It means that he preferred this world over his religion.

If Shurayḥ had acted differently, he might've changed history. If he had told the people that Hāniʾ was alive but imprisoned and that ʿUbayd Allah b. Ziyād was bent on killing him, they would've attacked the palace, saved Hāniʾ, grew bolder, and captured Ibn Ziyād and killed or banished him. This is because Ibn Ziyād did not have the upper hand yet. Kūfa would've been ready to receive Imām al-Ḥusayn ﷺ and the Battle of Karbalāʾ wouldn't have happened. If the Battle of Karbalāʾ hadn't happened, Imām al-Ḥusayn ﷺ would have come into power. Even if his rule lasted five short months—and it might've lasted a lot longer—it would've had a great positive effect on human history.

A movement may sometimes change the face of history. However, a miscalculated movement that comes out of fear, weakness, worldliness, and greed drags history into the abyss of perdition. You, Qāḍī Shurayḥ, why didn't you bear witness to the truth when you saw Hāniʾ's condition? This is the effect of elites who prefer the world over their religion.

When Ibn Ziyād ordered the notables of the tribes to go and work on driving the people away from Muslim, why did they obey him? They weren't all Umayyads; they hadn't come from Shām. Some of them, such as Shabath b. Ribʿī, personally wrote letters to Imām al-Ḥusayn ﷺ asking him to come to Kūfa! Shabath b. Ribʿī was one of the people whom Ibn Ziyād ordered to disperse the people, so he went and used threats, intimidations, and temptations. Why did they act like this?

If someone like Shabath b. Ribʿī feared God ﷻ for one crucial moment instead of fearing Ibn Ziyād, he would have changed history. Instead, these people dedicated themselves to discouraging others, so the masses dispersed. The question that poses itself is this: "Why did the faithful elites who were with Muslim disperse as well?" Among these elites were good, righteous people, and some of them went to Karbalāʾ afterward and were martyred there to atone for their mistake. I'm speaking of them generally without mentioning their names. There were also other elites who never went to Karbalāʾ. They were unable to or they did not have the chance, but they later joined the ranks of the penitents.

The Penitents' Effect on History

But what use is all that after the calamity of Karbalāʾ, the death of the Prophet's ﷺ grandson, and the beginning of history's downward spiral? The number of the penitents was manifold times that of the martyrs of Karbalāʾ. The martyrs of Karbalāʾ were all killed in one day, and the penitents were also killed in one day. However, you notice that the penitents' effect on history is not one thousandth as strong as the effect of martyrs of Karbalāʾ. This is because the penitents did not embark on their duty at the right time, and their decision came too late. Why did they leave Muslim, the messenger of Imām al-Ḥusayn ؑ, alone after they had pledged allegiance to him? I'm not talking about the masses here but about the elites. Why did they leave him no place of refuge when the darkness of the night engulfed him except Ṭawʿa's house?

The Inaction of the Elites Towards Muslim b. ʿAqil

Imagine that the elites hadn't abandoned Muslim and that a hundred men hid him in the houses of one of them and defended him. When ʿUbayd Allah b. Ziyād's men came to arrest Muslim when he was left alone, he resisted for several hours and managed to thwart them despite their great numbers and although they attacked him many times. Had he had a hundred men with him, would they have managed to capture him? No, because people would have rushed to their aid.

This means that the elites failed to fulfill their duty when they didn't rush to help Muslim. Wherever we look, we notice incidents that concern the elites. This means that if the elites make a decision at the right time, denounce the world in the right moment, and hold to the path of God ﷻ when the chance comes, they will save history and preserve values. In other words, the right decision must be made at the right time. If a decision is made too late, it will be pointless.

After the Algerian elections in which the Islamic Salvation Front (FIS) won, the army took control at the instigation of America and other powers. From the first day of the military government, it had no power. If the officials of the FIS led the people to the streets from day one, they would have defeated that government and established an Islamic rule in Algeria. This was because the military government wasn't very powerful back then. I said this to the officials of the FIS themselves. However, they did not make such a decision: some were afraid, others were weak, and some of them responded by fighting over the identity of the leader.

Imām Khumaynī's Firm Decision

On the afternoon of 21 Bahman of the year 1357 SH (1979 AD), martial law was declared in Tehran, but the Imām called on the people to take to the streets. Had he not made that decision at that moment, Mohammad Reza would have still controlled this country. If the people stayed home when martial law was declared, Mohammad Reza's men would have gone after the Imām, Refah School, and then the rest of Iran. They would've killed five-hundred thousand people in Tehran alone, and everything would have been over. This happened in Indonesia: those in power killed a million people and things went back to the way they were. Their ruler has remained in power until today, and he is much esteemed. The Imām, however, took the right decision at the crucial moment.

If the elites had determined what needed to be done at the right moment and did it, they would have changed history, and the likes of Imām al-Ḥusayn b. 'Alī wouldn't have been forced to go to Karbalā'. Sometimes the elites misunderstand the situation or understand it too late. Sometimes they understand it but disagree among themselves, which is what happened with our brothers in Afghanistan. Those who take control may be competent but the elites may not cooperate with them, claiming that they were busy and or that the war was over and that it was time to move on and make a living. The elites might say that they were sick of fighting and running around from front to front. If they behave like this, know that what happened in Karbalā' will be repeated.

Are You of the Elites or the Masses?

God ﷻ has promised to grant victory to anyone who fights for Him. If anyone rises up for God ﷻ and makes an effort, victory will be his. I don't mean that each person will be individually granted victory but that any group that decides to fight will be granted victory. Naturally, its path will include hardship, death, and pain, but it will include victory too.

God ﷻ says, "God will surely help those who help Him." He does not say We will help you while you remain unharmed. No. He says they "kill and are killed." In the end, however, they will be victorious. This is a divine precept (*sunna ilāhiyya*). Fear for our lives, dignities, money, families, loved ones, comfort, and ease, and our greed for money and luxurious houses hamper our movement. In this case, even if people like

Imām al-Ḥusayn ﷺ were leading the way, they would have been martyred just like Imām al-Ḥusayn and Imām ʿAlī ﷺ were martyred.

The Elites, the Elites, the Elite Class

Dear ones, consider where you stand. If you are truly of the elites, then beware. This is all we wish to say. Our discussion is a consequence of this topic that deserves to be examined on two levels. The first level is the historical level. If I had more time, I would have discussed it myself, but unfortunately, I'm out of time. This aspect needs to be researched to highlight the many examples of elites in history, and the times when they were supposed to act but didn't, naming each of them. If our time allowed and a longer discussion wouldn't have tired us, I would've spoken for a whole hour about this topic. I can think of many examples.

Historical Incidents Applicable During All Eras

The second level of discussion is practical application in all eras. I don't only mean our time but during every era that the elites needed to fulfill their obligations but didn't. Another thing that needs to be discussed in this regard is that the elites should not be lured by the temptations of this world. We must not give in to this world, and I will give examples.

Dear ones, walking on the path of God ﷻ will always include opposition. If one of these elites had actually wanted to do something, the other elites would have blamed him and spoken harshly to him. This used to happen during the days of our Revolution, but the elites are obligated to resist such influences. This is one instance of the elites' jihād; they should withstand blame and harsh words because their opposers will always hurl accusations and abuse them.

Our Greatest Desire is Martyrdom

I ask God to guide you all and to muster Imām Khumaynī ﵀ with the prophets and Authorities of God. I ask Him to steady the Iranian people on this clear path.

O God, keep us alive to serve the Islamic Revolution and Islamic values, and let our deaths be on this path.

O God, make our deaths be martyrdoms in Your path, and elevate the ranks of our righteous martyrs day after day.

O God, give those who made sacrifices of us great reward and grant them full health and safety.

O God, grant the highest ranks to those who withstood hardships in this path, and those who had been held in captivity for a long time and were set free. O God, grant the highest ranks to those who have not been set free yet and to those who went missing or whose bodies were lost without a trace. O God, grant their families reward and patience.

O God, for the sake of Muḥammad and his family ﷺ show us Your might and power in humiliating and defeating all poles of arrogance. O God, let the Iranian people taste the sweetness of victory over them all.

O God, answer the needs of all Muslims, save Islamic countries from the claws of foreigners. O God, wake the leaders of the Islamic world from their slumbers of obliviousness, and save them from the swamps of appetites.

O God, as You have exterminated the USSR, we ask You to exterminate the other poles of arrogance.

O God, include in Your mercy and blessings everyone who lived and died on this path.

O God, accept, in Your kindness and generosity, all our deeds and efforts.

The Difficulties in Distinguishing Truth from Falsehood[32]

Distinguishing truth from falsehood has been one of the most difficult things across the history of humanity, and particularly the history of prophetic missions. Everyone wants to commit to the truth, practice it, and avoid falsehood except those who have become an object of God's ﷻ wrath and became manifestations of the Devil. Most people, people who are wise, fair, and humane, would like to avoid falsehood and commit to the truth, but determining the truth is not always an easy thing.

In one of Imām ʿAlī's ؑ sermons where he vents his sorrows, he states this plainly. He says, "If falsehood were removed from the truth, those who aspire to it would not mistake it, and if the truth were purified of the ambiguities of falsehood, those who oppose it would be silenced about it. But a measure of falsehood and a measure of truth are taken and mixed; this is how the Devil takes hold of his followers."[33]

We have suffered the consequences of confusing the truth and falsehood time and time again across

[32] *Ḥadīth al-Wilāya*, Vol. 2, p. 189, 190.

[33] al-Sharīf al-Raḍī, Muḥammad ibn al-Ḥusayn, Nahj al-Balāgha, Sermon/Letter/Saying 50.

prophetic and Islamic history. Colonialism and its evils have persisted for two centuries in our country. One of the reasons for the prolonged unrest in this country is perhaps this confusion between truth and falsehood and the absence of a clear path for the umma. This might be why we have been unable to strike the colonizers once and for all and prevent their return. The Iranian people have experienced one shock after another due to the confusion of truth and falsehood, whether during the Constitutional Revolution or the periods preceding and succeeding it.

The movement of the scholars and the people led by Imām Khumaynī قدس سره raised slogans that left no possibility of confusion. Truth and falsehood were separated after the people gradually knew the truth over fifteen years, distinguishing it from falsehood, and the Revolution was victorious. After the Revolution's victory, the Imām قدس سره, with the blood of prophet ʿĪsā عليه السلام running through his veins, did not allow the truth to be mixed with falsehood.

The Standard for Truth and Falsehood

If it's so easy to mix up truth and falsehood, there must be standards to distinguish them. God ﷻ would never leave people without landmarks and guideposts, so what is the standard that distinguishes truth from falsehood? We must search for it in the Qurʾān, narrations, and the words of the greats and the Authorities of God ﷻ. The

Qur'ān and the Prophetic sunna declare that everything that agrees with the Sharia belongs to the truth and everything that contradicts it belongs to falsehood. However, this standard is not readily available for all people to use given the difficulty of determining the dictates of the Sharia.

Narrow-mindedness and the Khawārij[34]

The Khawārij and the Error of the Elites

When concentration in worship (*tawajjuh*) is gone and the spirit of worship—which entails obedience, intimacy (*uns*) with God ﷻ, and submitting to Him ﷻ —is lost, man will be susceptible to many dangers. One of them is narrow-mindedness.

Some of the Khawārij, and you've been hearing about them a lot lately, eagerly worshipped God ﷻ, recited the Qur'ān, and performed their prayers. This caused some of Imām 'Alī's ؑ companions to be swayed by them. In the Battle of the Camel, one of Imām 'Alī's ؑ companions found one of the Khawārij engrossed in worship, reciting the Qur'ān melodiously in the middle of the night: "Is he who supplicates in the watches of the night..."[35] Imām 'Alī's ؑ companion was seized by

[34] *Ḥadīth al-Wilāya*, Vol. 4, p. 136-139.

[35] Sūrat al-Zumar, Verse 9.

doubt and came to the Imām and asked him about it. Even the conscious, close followers of Imām 'Alī ﷺ were susceptible to error.

Faith, Consciousness, and Imām 'Alī's ﷺ Sword

Imām 'Alī ﷺ said, "Do not kill the Khawārij after me. Those who sought the truth but mistook it are not like those who sought falsehood and attained it." He did not say this for nothing.

The situation required Imām 'Alī's ﷺ sword, Imām 'Alī's ﷺ consciousness, and Imām 'Alī's ﷺ confidence in himself and his path. Even the elites of his companions slipped sometimes.

According to a narration, Imām 'Alī ﷺ told his companion who was mentioned earlier, "I will tell you tomorrow." When the battle was over and only ten Khawārij were left, Imām 'Alī ﷺ walked among the dead and spoke to them to teach his companions a lesson. When he got to one of them, who was lying face down, Imām 'Alī ﷺ told his companions, "Turn him over" or perhaps he said, "Sit him up." Anyway, Imām 'Alī ﷺ asked his doubting companion, "Do you recognize him?" He responded, "No, O Commander of the Believers." Imām 'Alī ﷺ told him, "This is the man you saw reciting the Qur'ān yesterday!"

What recitation is this? What worship is this? This is a departure from the spirit of worship. The truth and essence of Islam are manifest in ʿAlī b. Abī Ṭālib ﷺ. Those who know the spirit of worship, prayer, and the Qurʾān would and join ʿAlī ﷺ without confusion. When a person cannot distinguish truth and falsehood and raises his sword in the face of ʿAlī ﷺ, he would be doing nothing but departing from religion and the Qurʾān.

The issue relates to narrow-mindedness, foolishness, and the horrible mistakes of the Umayyads and the Abbasids. Some people were considered saintly, pious, worshipful, and abstinent, but they made the mistake of confusing truth and falsehood. This is one of the greatest mistakes. Some mistakes cannot be forgiven, and one of them is confusing truth and falsehood.

Imām ʿAlī's ﷺ Closest Companions Never Made Mistakes

The greatness of ʿAmmār and his likes from the elite companions of Imām ʿAlī ﷺ lay in the fact that they were never confused or made mistakes. I observed this greatness in various instances during the Battle of Ṣiffīn. Of course, this greatness was not limited to Ṣiffīn. In times when the faithful were susceptible to confusion, there were people who had penetrating insights and eloquence, and who removed doubts from people's minds.

Throughout the events that Imām ʿAlī ﷺ participated in, including Ṣiffīn, we can always sense presence of this great, clear-sighted man called ʿAmmār b. Yāsir.

The Battle of Ṣiffīn lasted for months, and it was an amazing battle. People were observing their opponents praying, worshipping, reading the Qur'ān, and even raising their Qur'āns on spears. Courageous hearts are needed to fight such people.

A narration from Imām Jaʿfar al-Ṣādiq ﷺ states that if Imām ʿAlī ﷺ hadn't fought other Muslims, the obligation to fight tyrannical and sinful Muslims would have never been known in the Islamic world. ʿAlī b. Abī Ṭālib ﷺ established this path and clarified the obligation.

When our sons used to attack the enemies' fronts and take captives, they would find prayer beads and Ḥusaynī soil with them. These people are like the ones who stood against Imām ʿAlī ﷺ while performing their prayers. This almost tricked some people, but ʿAmmār b. Yāsir would always save them. The situation requires consciousness and intelligence like ʿAmmār b. Yāsir's.

If the spirit of deeds and acts of worship were unclear for someone — meaning concentration and worship of God ﷻ — this makes this person unable to draw near to God ﷻ with his deeds. All his deeds would be superficial, and superficial faith and deeds are always precarious. I have observed this throughout Islamic history.

The Power of Falsehood

I already spoke of faithful, saintly, and abstinent people who used to attend the courts of some tyrannical and immoral caliphs. These caliphs were hypocritical and two faced. When given advice and counsel, they would be moved, either genuinely or out of hypocrisy and falsity. Some caliphs would even be drunk at the time of counsel. They would get seized by feeling and emotion, sometimes to the extent of crying. This caused naïve people, despite their apparent knowledge of religion, to become part of the caliphs' entourage!

There are marvelous examples in Islamic history. One of them is 'Amr b. 'Ubayd. He was known for his worship and piety. The Abbasid caliph said about him, "All of you are watchful and anticipating to gain something except 'Amr b. 'Ubayd." This means that 'Amr b. 'Ubayd was different from all those who claimed to be abstinent and pious. Let us compare this man to Muḥammad b. Shihāb al-Zuhrī and his ilk. The latter worked against the truth and supported falsehood, leaving the truth that is represented by Ahl al-Bayt عليهم السلام, oppressed and alone. Due to these people's ignorance, the enemy was able to breach Islam.

Destroying Inner Idols

The spirit of worship is obedience to God ﷻ. Brothers and sisters, we must strive to awaken the spirit of obedience within ourselves. We must submit to God ﷻ and destroy the idol that lies within each one of us.

Obliviousness and Confusion Destroy Righteous Deeds[36]

The Secret to the Imām's ؒ Actions

The Imām's ؒ secret that captivated the hearts of people and turned the world upside down is his steady wayfaring toward perfection. Me and my likes have a problem understanding that and applying it. It is easy to speak of, but applying it is difficult. We cannot even understand this but Imām Khumaynī ؒ actually applied it. Don't think that the Imām ؒ who passed to the vicinity of his Lord in 1368 SH (1989 AD) was the same man who came to Tehran in 1357 SH (1979 AD). No, the Imām ؒ moved forward and rose to new heights.

It's true that we cannot reach the ranks of that great man ؒ, but when we look at him from below, we see the height at which he was soaring. God ﷻ is my witness: when I used to visit the Imām ؒ after every

[36] *Ḥadīth al-Wilāya*, Vol. 6, p. 248-251.

Ramaḍān, I felt that he rose more and more above material things every time. He was becoming more perfect day after day, and every believer should be like this: The man who has two equal days that are the same (where there is no change in his character or his deeds) is indeed a loser. And whoever is worse by the day, then he is cursed."[37]

Bad Deeds Suppress Faith

Many people fought under the Prophet ﷺ but could not preserve their past record. Imām ʿAlī ؑ said about the sword of that man who always fought under the Prophet ﷺ but eventually was killed in battle, "This is a sword that had long kept distress away from the Prophet's ﷺ face."[38]

Suddenly, that very same sword was raised in the face of ʿAlī b. Abī Ṭālib ؑ! This means that we must preserve our record; we are also susceptible to failure: "They are the ones whose works have failed."[39] This means that their deeds were all for nothing. Don't think that if we did a good deed it will stay on our record even if we do bad deeds. No; bad deeds drive away good deeds when

---

[37] al-Majlisī, al-ʿAllamah Muḥammad Bāqir, *Biḥār al-Anwār*, Vol. 70, p. 173.

[38] Translator's note: This is a reference to al-Zubayr b. al-ʿAwwām.

[39] Sūrat al-Tawba, Verse 69.

we stand before God ﷻ. Bad deeds sometimes even destroy the faith entirely: "Then the fate of those who committed misdeeds was that they denied the signs of God."[40]

There are people like this among us. I know people who used to do good deeds but strayed and fell due to obliviousness, confusion, greed, and entitlement. This is a hole that opens up in the straight path, and it's very dangerous. Although it may be small, it will gradually get bigger and away from the straight path. The people I mentioned got to a point when they did things that opposed the Revolution, Islam, and the Islamic order, although they had once been servants of Islam and the Revolution.

Who is to Blame?

Some people think that the Revolution is blameworthy because it did not retain these people in its ranks, but this is wrong. The truth is this: "So do not blame me, but blame yourselves."[41] Those who embraced Islam did not do a favor to Islam; similarly, a revolutionary did not do a favor to the Revolution. God ﷻ tells His Prophet ﷺ: "They count it as a favor to *you* that they have embraced Islam. *Say*, 'Do not count it as a favor to

---

[40] Sūrat al-Rūm, Verse 10.

[41] Sūrat Ibrāhīm, Verse 22.

me your embracing of Islam. Rather it is God who has done you a favor in that He has guided you to faith..."[42] God ﷻ has done us all a favor in guiding us to Islam.

Many people in our world today are misguided and selfish. Many youths in our so-called civilized world are like animals, paying attention to nothing but their lowly physical needs. Animals are like that, whereas humans determine their aims using logic, reason, and honorable emotions. After that, they move toward those aims wholeheartedly and disregard any obstacles. The U.S., Europe, and other countries that are subject to tyranny are full of such youths.

We Must Preserve Islam

You should thank God ﷻ for guiding you to pure faith and authentic monotheism. God ﷻ gave us character and independence. The powers controlling the world today do not know the worship of God ﷻ; rather, they consider people as their slaves. What's worse is that the people themselves have accepted this. These powers only fear countries that refuse to be subjugated by them. You haven't always been like this yourselves; Islam made you like this. You have to know the value of Islam. We must not think that our achievement will simply last forever; we must actively strive to preserve it.

[42] Sūrat al-Ḥujurāt, Verse 17.

A Last Word in Lamenting the Master of the Martyrs, Imām al-Ḥusayn ﷺ[43]

Peace Be Upon You, O Abā 'Abdillāh ﷺ

Today, I would like to read excerpts to you from Ibn Ṭawūs' *al-Luhūf* so that we can look at some amazing scenes together. This is a very trustworthy book written by Sayyid 'Alī b. Ṭawūs who is an honest, trustworthy, and respected scholar, jurist, and mystic. He was a teacher to some great jurists, aside from being a man of letters, a poet, and an esteemed person. He wrote the first trustworthy and brief maqtal. *Al-Luhūf* was preceded by many books on the death of Imām al-Ḥusayn ﷺ. Even his teacher Ibn Namā wrote a maqtal, and Shaykh al-Ṭūsī wrote one too. By writing *al-Luhūf*, Ibn Ṭawūs eclipsed other maqātil. The reason for this was Ibn Ṭawūs' esteem, accuracy, and brevity.

Al-Qāsim b. al-Ḥasan

One of the scenes he depicts for us is al-Qāsim b. al-Ḥasan going to battle. It is an extremely touching scene. Al-Qāsim was an underage boy. On the eve of the tenth of Muḥarram, Imām al-Ḥusayn ﷺ told his companions that the battle was inevitable and that they would all be killed. He gave them permission to leave, but they

[43] Sayyid Khāmina'ī's Friday prayer sermon in Tehran on 18/2/1377 SH.

refused to do so. This thirteen or fourteen-year-old boy asked his uncle Imām al-Ḥusayn ﷺ whether he would be killed too. Imām al-Ḥusayn ﷺ wanted to test him, so he asked, "How do you see death?" Al-Qāsim's response was, "Sweeter than honey."

Notice: these are the values that Ahl al-Bayt ﷺ and their children had. This boy was three or four years old when his father Imām al-Ḥasan was martyred, so Imām al-Ḥusayn ﷺ took it upon himself to raise him. On the eve of the tenth of Muḥarram, this boy stood by his uncle. Ibn Ṭawūs says, "The narrator said, 'A boy as beautiful as the moon went out and began fighting.'"

The narrators have recorded the incidents of the tenth day of Muḥarram in detail, mentioning the names of those who struck and those who were stricken, the first person to shoot an arrow, and the names of those who pillaged and robbed. Among these names, they mentioned the name of the man who stole Imām al-Ḥusayn's ﷺ garment; he was known from then on as "the garment thief (*sāriq al-qaṭīfa*)." This means that Ahl al-Bayt ﷺ and those who love them did not let this incident be forgotten.

The narrator says, "Ibn Fuḍayl al-Azdī struck al-Qāsim on his head and cut it open, so the boy fell and called out, 'Uncle!' Imām al-Ḥusayn ﷺ rushed like a falcon and attacked like an angry lion, striking Ibn Fuḍayl with his sword and killing him. The people of Kūfa rushed in to save him but Imām al-Ḥusayn عليه السلام fought them off." A battle raged at the spot where al-Qāsim b. al-Ḥasan was killed, and Imām al-Ḥusayn عليه السلام defeated them all.

The narrator continues, "When the dust of the battle settled, I saw al-Ḥusayn عليه السلام standing at the head of the boy who was moving his legs. al-Ḥusayn عليه السلام was saying, "Woe to the people who killed you." It's a wondrous, heart-wrenching scene that reflects Imām al-Ḥusayn's عليه السلام tender heart and his love for this boy as well as his sacrifice. His sacrifice lies in the fact that he gave al-Qāsim permission to fight. This incident also reflects the boy's greatness of spirit and his enemies' hard-heartedness.

ʿAlī al-Akbar Goes to Battle

Another scene is ʿAlī al-Akbar heading to battle. It really is a moving scene from all angles. It's touching from the viewpoints of Imām al-Ḥusayn عليه السلام, ʿAlī al-Akbar himself, and the women, and particularly his aunt Sayyidah Zaynab al-Kubrā عليها السلام. The sources mention that ʿAlī al-Akbar was between eighteen and twenty-five years old.

The narrator says, "ʿAlī al-Akbar came out to battle. He was the handsomest and politest of people. He asked his father permission to fight and was allowed." It's narrated that when al-Qāsim b. al-Ḥasan عليه السلام wanted to fight, al-Ḥusayn عليه السلام allowed it only after al-Qāsim insisted. However, ʿAlī b. al-Ḥusayn ؑ was his own son, so he gave him permission immediately "and then he looked at him like one who has lost hope in his return and cried."

This is one of the merits of the Muslims, as they shed tears in emotional moments. You notice that Imām al-Ḥusayn ؑ cried more than once. He was not crying out of fear but out of deep emotion. Islam cultivates this emotion in people. After his conversation with ʿAlī al-Akbar, Imām al-Ḥusayn ؑ said, "God be our witness; a young man most like your Prophet in appearance, manners, and speech came out to battle these people."

Here, I would like to tell you something. During his childhood, Imām al-Ḥusayn ؑ was much loved by the Prophet ﷺ, and he also loved his grandfather ﷺ dearly. When the Prophet ﷺ passed away, Imām al-Ḥusayn ؑ was six or seven years old. The Prophet ﷺ remained etched on his mind and rooted in his heart. Later in life, God ﷻ granted Imām al-Ḥusayn ؑ ʿAlī al-Akbar. The days passed, and the son grew to resemble the Prophet ﷺ, so Imām al-Ḥusayn's ؑ heart was seized by love for him equal to his love for the Prophet ﷺ. This young man resembled the Prophet ﷺ in his appearance, features, voice, speech, and manners, and he bore that same generosity and honor.

Imām al-Ḥusayn ؑ continued talking and said, "O God, whenever we missed your Prophet, we used to look at him [ʿAlī al-Akbar]" then he yelled, "O Ibn Saʿd, may God cut off your blood relations like you're cutting off mine!" ʿAlī al-Akbar went out and fought fiercely, killing many. He went back to his father and said, "O father, I'm dying of thirst, and the weight of the armor has left me exhausted. Is there any water to be had?"

Imām al-Ḥusayn ﷺ responded, "Fight a little longer. Soon you will meet your grandfather Muḥammad ﷺ and he will quench your thirst with a drink from his perfect cup, and you will never know thirst again." ʿAlī al-Akbar went back to the battlefield and fought with all his heart, and when he was hit, he called out, "Peace upon you, father. My grandfather sends you his salutations and tells you, 'make haste in coming to us.'"

Imām al-Ḥusayn's ﷺ Movement Saved Human History

These are horrible scenes from that immortal battle. On this day, the eleventh of Muḥarram, the day of Sayyidah Zaynab al-Kubrā ﷺ, atrocious things happened. From the moment Imām al-Ḥusayn ﷺ was martyred, Sayyidah Zaynab al-Kubrā ﷺ took it upon herself to bear that heavy trust. She walked that path with unmatched courage and strength, as a daughter of Imām ʿAlī ﷺ should. They all walked this path, immortalizing Islam and preserving the features of religion. The Battle of al-Ṭaff did not save one umma or one group of people; it saved the whole of humanity. Imām al-Ḥusayn ﷺ, his sister Sayyidah Zaynab al-

Kubrā عليها السلام, his household, and his companions saved human history through their heroic stances.

Peace be upon you, O Abā ʿAbdillāh عليه السلام and upon the souls that gathered in your courtyard. Peace of God be upon you from me forever, as long as I may live and as long as there are day and night. May God not make this my last visit to you. Peace be upon al-Ḥusayn, and upon ʿAlī b. al-Ḥusayn, and upon the sons of al-Ḥusayn, and upon the companions of al-Ḥusayn.

O God, we ask You by Muḥammad and the household of Muḥammad to steady us in your religion and the rulings of Your Book.

O God, make our society an Islamic society.

O God, do not separate us from Islam.

O God, grant victory to Islam and the Muslims all over the earth, and fail the enemies of Islam.

O God, spread among us the values of Islam, the ties of brotherhood, love, and worship, as well as complete justice.

O God, thwart by Your mercy all the enemies who seek to distance our society from Islam.

O God, please the heart of the Master of the Age, Imām al-Mahdī عجّل الله تعالى فرجه الشريف, may our souls be ransom for him, make us of his supporters and helpers, and answer his prayers for our people.

O God, bestow Your mercy upon our dear martyrs, the Imām of the Martyrs Imām al-Ḥusayn عليه السلام, and all those who made sacrifices.

www.ingramcontent.com/pod-product-compliance
Lightning Source LLC
Chambersburg PA
CBHW021442070526
44577CB00002B/254
9781956276046